Louis Freeland Post

Outlines of Louis F. Post's lectures

On, The single Tax, Absolute free Trade, The Labor Question, etc.

Louis Freeland Post

Outlines of Louis F. Post's lectures
On, The single Tax, Absolute free Trade, The Labor Question, etc.

ISBN/EAN: 9783337132859

Printed in Europe, USA, Canada, Australia, Japan

Cover: Foto ©ninafisch / pixelio.de

More available books at **www.hansebooks.com**

LOUIS F. POST'S LECTURES.

TESTIMONIALS FROM EDUCATIONAL INSTITUTIONS.

" I doubt if the school ever enjoyed any lectures on political economy as much as yours, because you presented the subject with such simplicity and clearness that even the most immature minds could follow it."—*Sara M. Ely, of The Misses Ely's School, Riverside Drive, Eighty-fifth and Eighty-sixth Streets, New York.*

" It is the unanimous verdict of the most competent judges, that this lecture of Mr. Post's is not only the best which has so far been delivered, but shows extraordinary power of clear and instructive exposition of his theory and of the fundamental principles of economics. He impressed every intelligent person with the conviction that he was a very remarkable teacher." —*J. A. Quarles, D.D., LL.D., Professor of Moral Philosophy, Washington and Lee University, Lexington, Va.*

" I had the pleasure of hearing in the chapel of Washington and Lee University the lecture of Mr. Post on single tax. I was greatly impressed by the ability of the lecturer, and thought that I had never heard a more simple, full, and clear exposition of the principles of the science upon which the deductions of the lecturer were based. Mr. Post has most admirable and exceptional gifts as a lecturer and a teacher."—*Gen. Scott Shipp, Superintendent Virginia Military Institute, Lexington, Va.*

" Mr. Post's lecture in City Hall last evening on ' Progress and Poverty ' demonstrated that the elementary truths of political economy can be presented to an audience in a simple, luminous and deeply interesting way."—*Edwin P. Wentworth, ex-President Maine Chautauqua Union.*

" Mr. Post is a clear and pleasing speaker. He is thoroughly familiar with the single tax theory. He states his case in a clear and convincing manner. He was especially satisfactory in the exposition of the single tax theory, which he gave to the class in answer to questions by members of the class."—*Prof. Jesse Macy, Chair of Constitutional History and Political Economy, Iowa College, Grinnell, Ia.*

" I was an interested listener at Mr. Post's last lecture in Seattle. I did not miss a word, nor lose a thought. While not accepting all his doctrine, I believe he has no superior on the platform to-day."—*Thomas M. Gatch, President of the University of the State of Washington, Seattle, Wash.*

LETTERS FROM REPRESENTATIVE MEN.

" Mr. Post's method of presenting the subject of political economy is admirable. His charts and diagrams, together with his clear, concise, and forcible manner of presenting the subject, make his lectures exceedingly entertaining and instructive."—*E. H. Long, Superintendent of Public Schools of St. Louis, Mo.*

" I not only enjoyed your lecture immensely, but think that any one who had the vaguest interest in social questions could not help being pleased with it."—*Bolton Hall, New York City.*

" I am not satisfied to let you leave Boston without an expression of my enjoyment of your admirable lectures. The approving words that have since come to me from many listeners are an assurance that my opinion is unbiased."—*Wm. Lloyd Garrison, Boston, Mass.*

" Wherever my endorsement may be of any use to you I will be glad unequivocally to give it—to your personal character, to your ability as a writer and lecturer, and to the soundness, from my point of view, of the single tax doctrines you are so successfully teaching."—*Henry George.*

EXTRACTS FROM NEWSPAPER REPORTS AND EDITORIALS.

" Mr. Post is eloquent and entertaining."—*San Francisco (Cal.) Chronicle.*

" Mr. Post is a speaker of much magnetism. His lecture was replete with anecdote, and abounded in humor and illustration."—*Los Angeles (Cal.) Express.*

" He is not rhetorical ; uses plain, simple language, and is a natural logician. A subject complicated to many was made simple and clear by his instructive discourse."—*Waco (Tex.) Evening News.*

" He is an orator, but his style is conversational. . . His language was so clear that even a child could understand."—*El Paso (Tex.) Daily Times.*

" There was not a dry nor uninteresting moment in the whole discourse."—*San Francisco (Cal.) Star.*

EXTRACTS FROM NEWSPAPERS.

"Mr. Post's success in the treatment of his subject lies in the charm of his manner. He talks to his audience, never tiring them, surprising them by apt and unexpected contrasts and illustrations, and running in his explanatory anecdotes with a fluency and dry humor which sustain interest until the last word. . . . He never spared hypocrisy, winked at dishonesty, or tolerated any means of redress for wrongs except by peaceable and logical means."—*Seattle (Wash.) Post-Intelligencer*.

"Mr. Post's style was admirable, his utterance rapid, and he crowded into the compass of a single lecture enough to make a volume."—*Raton (N. M.) Reporter*.

"Mr. Post is a clear speaker, not lacking in platform readiness and wit."—*Montreal Herald*.

"Mr. Louis F. Post is a clear, logical, and extremely careful speaker."—*Montreal Witness*.

"A fluent speaker, and states his points very clearly."—*Toronto Empire*.

"Mr. Post's style is lucid and forcible, without anything savoring of grandiloquence."—*Vancouver (B. C.) Daily News-Advertiser*.

"He is a splendid speaker, clear, forcible, uses no notes, and besides, is possessed of the gift of humor, which he brings into welcome play."—*Nanaimo (B. C.) Free Press*.

"The large audience was delighted with the lecture, notwithstanding the fact that many of the ideas advanced were new and strange to the greater part."—*Aspen (Col.) Daily Times*.

"He is a pleasing and effective speaker, and understands his subject so thoroughly that he easily gained and held the attention of his entire audience from the beginning to the close of his lecture."—*Mascoutah (Ill.) Herald*.

"A very pleasing speaker, easy and natural, with excellent voice and convincing manner."—*Elgin (Ill.) Daily News*.

"Mr. Post is an ideal lecturer."—*Sioux City (Ia.) Journal*.

"Mr. Post is one of the most forcible speakers heard in Des Moines on any subject in a long time."—*Des Moines (Ia.) Saturday Review*.

"Louis F. Post turned what would ordinarily be a dry, abstract discussion, in which only special students would be interested, into a dissertation which all could understand, and by which all could profit."—*Dubuque (Ia.) Herald*.

"An admirable presentation of the single tax doctrine."—*Cedar Rapids (Ia.) Republican*.

"Mr. Post is a very entertaining talker, and is thoroughly versed in political economy."—*Atchison (Kan.) Globe*.

"For two and one-half hours he held the attention of his audience, interest in the subject increasing at every stage of his address."—*New Iberia (La.) Enterprise*.

"Held his audience as by the power of a master mind."—*New Iberia (La.) Daily Iberian*.

"A masterpiece of earnest eloquence and logical argument."—*Boston (Mass.) Advertiser*.

"Has a power of clear and graphic presentation which few men possess."—*Editorial in Boston (Mass.) Herald*.

"The exposition of the Henry George theory was entertainingly clear, and furnishes a good basis for future thought upon the subject."—*University of Michigan Daily, Ann Arbor*.

"The lecture—it was more of a talk—was really a primer lesson on government and taxation. It was quietly and earnestly given in plain words."—*Detroit (Mich.) Tribune*.

"The lecturer is one of the best on the American platform."—*Cadillac (Mich.) State Democrat*.

"Mr. Post strikes one as being a deep thinker, a scholar, a gentleman, and an unostentatious talker who loses sight of himself in the interest he feels in the subject he is presenting."—*Adrian (Mich.) Daily Times*.

"Mr. Post is a very attractive and convincing speaker, and the impression he made upon all who heard his address last night was most favorable, and undoubtedly gave dignity and won intellectual respect for his cause from many persons who have not heretofore been disposed to give it serious consideration."—*Editorial in Minneapolis (Minn.) Times*.

"Mr. Post is evidently much more interested in impressing his audience with the theory he elaborates than with himself as its exponent. His gestures are a secondary consideration, and his appearance is that of a professor before his class."—*Kansas City (Mo.) Times*.

"The address was two hours and a half in delivery, but was so clear and logical that it was listened to with great interest."—*Lincoln (Neb.) State Journal*.

"His oratory held the attention of the audience throughout his lecture."—*Buffalo (N. Y.) Enquirer*.

"He delighted his hearers by his lucid treatment of the theme."—*Philadelphia (Pa.) Record*.

"A fluent and entertaining talker, and speaks entirely without notes. He intersperses his arguments and solid points with illustrations in the shape of luminous anecdotes."—*Galveston (Tex.) Daily News*.

"An interesting speaker, and his lecture was occasionally varied by a bright epigram or laughable anecdote that gave pungency to his speech."—*Spokane (Wash.) Chronicle*.

"Mr. Post is a clear and forcible speaker, and presents the Henry George theory of taxation with fine effect."—*Christian Standard*.

OF

LOUIS F. POST'S LECTURES

ON

THE SINGLE TAX

ABSOLUTE FREE TRADE

THE LABOR QUESTION

PROGRESS AND POVERTY

THE LAND QUESTION

THE ELEMENTS OF POLITICAL ECONOMY

SOCIALISM

HARD TIMES

With Illustrative Notes and Charts

NEW YORK
THE STERLING LIBRARY
106 FULTON STREET

CONTENTS.

DIVISION		PAGE
	PREFATORY NOTE,	1
I.	THE SINGLE TAX DEFINED,	1
II.	THE SINGLE TAX AS A FISCAL REFORM,	4
	1. DIRECT AND INDIRECT TAXATION,	4
	2. THE TWO KINDS OF DIRECT TAXATION,	7
	(1) In proportion to ability to pay; and (2) in proportion to benefits received.	
	3. THE SINGLE TAX FALLS IN PROPORTION TO BENEFITS,	10
	4. CONFORMITY TO GENERAL PRINCIPLES OF TAXATION,	15
	a. INTERFERENCE WITH PRODUCTION,	16
	b. CHEAPNESS OF COLLECTION,	17
	c. CERTAINTY,	17
	d. EQUALITY,	19
III.	THE SINGLE TAX AS A SOCIAL REFORM,	20
	1. THE SOURCE OF WEALTH (Charts),	27
	2. THE PRODUCTION OF WEALTH,	37
	a. DIVISION OF LABOR (Charts),	40
	b. TRADE (Charts),	42
	c. THE LAW OF DIVISION OF LABOR AND TRADE (Charts),	45
	Note 72. Mechanism of Trade (Charts),	52
	d. DEPENDENCE OF LABOR UPON LAND (Chart),	59

DIVISION		PAGE
3. THE DISTRIBUTION OF WEALTH, ...		63
a. EXPLANATION OF WAGES AND RENT, .		66
b. NORMAL EFFECT OF SOCIAL PROGRESS UPON WAGES AND RENT, ...		72
c. SIGNIFICANCE OF THE UPWARD TENDENCY OF RENT, ...		74
d. EFFECT OF CONFISCATING RENT TO PRIVATE USE, ...		76
e. EFFECT OF RETAINING RENT FOR COMMON USE, ...		86
IV. CONCLUSION, ...		88
APPENDIX:		
BRIEF ANSWERS TO TYPICAL QUESTIONS, . .		91

OUTLINES OF POST'S LECTURES.

PREFATORY NOTE.

These "Outlines," while giving neither the substance nor the arrangement of any of the lectures named in the title, contain the leading points of all. But to make the points consecutive they have been woven into one of the lectures—that on the Single Tax. This, however, is not arbitrary, for the philosophy of the single tax involves the elementary principles of absolute free trade, of the labor question, of poverty with progress, of the land question, and of political economy; and while exposing the fallacies of socialism it explains the problem of hard times.

The "Outlines" do not take the place of the lectures. They are published merely to prepare the mind of the reader in advance to more fully appreciate the lectures during delivery, and to assist afterward in recalling and deliberately considering and criticizing what is advanced from the platform. To this end the principal charts of all the lectures are reproduced.

The text in large type is a connected explanation. It may be read and fully understood without reference to the notes. But the notes elaborate and illustrate points which, from the conciseness of their statement in the text, may seem obscure to readers who are unaccustomed to economic thought.

I. THE SINGLE TAX DEFINED.

The practical form in which Henry George puts the idea of appropriating economic rent to common use is "*To abolish all taxation save that upon land values.*"[1]

[1] "Progress and Poverty," book viii, ch. ii.

This is now generally known as "The Single Tax."[2] Under its operation all classes of workers, whether manufacturers, merchants, bankers, professional men, clerks, mechanics, farmers, farm-hands, or other working classes, would, *as such*, be wholly exempt. It is only as men own land that they would be taxed, the tax of each being in proportion, not to the area, but to the value of his land. And no one would be compelled to pay a higher tax than others if his land were improved or used while theirs was not, nor if his were better improved or better used than theirs.[3] The value

---

2. In "Progress and Poverty," book viii, ch. iv, Henry George speaks of "the effect of substituting for the manifold taxes now imposed, *a single tax* on the value of land"; but the term did not become a distinctive name until 1888.

The first general movement along the lines of "Progress and Poverty" began with the New York City election of 1886, when Henry George polled 68,110 votes as an independent candidate for mayor, and was defeated by the Democratic candidate, Abram S. Hewitt, by a plurality of only 22,442, the Republican, Theodore Roosevelt, polling but 60,435. Following that election the United Labor Party was formed, which at the Syracuse Convention in August, 1887, by the exclusion of the Socialists, came to represent the central idea of "Progress and Poverty" as distinguished from the Socialistic propaganda which until then was identified with it. Coincident with the organization of the United Labor Party the Anti-Poverty Society was formed; and the two bodies, one representing the political and the other the religious phase of the idea, worked together until President Cleveland's tariff message of 1887 appeared. In this message Mr. George saw the timid beginnings of that open struggle between protection and free trade to which he had for years looked forward as the political movement that must culminate in the abolition of all taxes save those upon land values, and he responded at once to the sentiments of the message. But many protectionists, who had followed him because they supposed he was a land nationalizer, now broke away from his leadership, and the United Labor Party and the Anti-Poverty Society were soon practically dissolved. Those who understood Mr. George's real position regarding the land question readily acquiesced in his views as to political policy, and a considerable movement resulted, which, however, for some time lacked an identifying name. This was the situation when Thomas G. Shearman, Esq., wrote for the *Standard* an article on taxation in which he illustrated and advocated the land value tax as a fiscal measure. The article had been submitted without a caption, and Mr. George, then the editor of the *Standard*, entitled it "The Single Tax." This title was at once adopted by the "George men," as they were often called, and has ever since served as the name of the movement it describes.

Though "the single tax" is the English form of "l'impôt unique," the name of the French physiocratic doctrine of the eighteenth century, the names have no historical connection, and they stand for different ideas.

3. When it is remembered that some land in cities is worth millions of dollars an acre, that a small building lot in the business center of even a small village is worth more than a whole field of the best farming land in the neighborhood, that a few acres

THE SINGLE TAX DEFINED. 3

of its improvements would not be considered in estimating the value of a holding ; site value alone would govern.' If a site rose in the market the tax would proportionately increase ; if that fell, the tax would proportionately diminish.

The single tax may be concisely described as a tax upon land alone, in the ratio of value, irrespective of improvements or use.

of coal or iron land are worth more than great groups of farms, that the right of way of a railroad company through a thickly settled district or between important points is worth more than its rolling stock, and that the value of workingmen's cottages in the suburbs is trifling in comparison with the value of city residence sites, the absurdity, if not the dishonesty, of the plea that the single tax would discriminate against farmers and small home owners and in favor of the rich is apparent. The bad faith of this plea is emphasized when we consider that under existing systems of taxation the farmer and the poor home owner are compelled to pay in taxes upon improvements, food, clothing, and other objects of consumption, much more than the full annual value of their bare land.

4. The difference between site value and improvement value is much more definite than it is often supposed to be. Even in what would seem at first to be most confusing cases, it is easily distinguished. If in any example we imagine the complete destruction of all the improvements, we may discover in the remaining value of the property—in the price it would after such destruction fetch in the real estate market—the value of the site as distinguished from the value of the improvements. This residuum of value would be the basis of computation for levying the single tax.

The distinction is frequently made in business life. Whenever in the course of ordinary business affairs it becomes necessary to estimate the value of a building lot, or to fix royalties for mining privileges, no difficulty is experienced, and substantial justice is done. And though the exigencies of business seldom require the site value of an improved farm to be distinguished from the value of its improvements, yet it could doubtless be done as easily and justly as with city or mining property. Unimproved land attached to any farm in question, or unimproved land in the neighborhood, if similar in fertility and location, would furnish a sufficiently accurate measure. If neither existed, the value of the contiguous highway would always be available.

It should not be forgotten that land for which the demand is so weak that its site value cannot be easily distinguished from the value of its improvements, is certain to be land of but little value, and almost certain to have no value at all.

The objection that the value of land cannot be distinguished from the value of its improvements is among the most frivolous of the objections that have been raised to the single tax by people with whom the wish that it may be impracticable is father to the thought that it really is so.

II. THE SINGLE TAX AS A FISCAL REFORM.

1. DIRECT AND INDIRECT TAXATION.

Taxes are either *direct* or *indirect;* or, as they have been aptly described, "straight" or "crooked." Indirect taxes are those that may be shifted by the first payer from himself to others; direct taxes are those that cannot be shifted.[5]

The shifting of indirect taxes is accomplished by means of their tendency to increase the prices of commodities upon which they fall. Their magnitude and incidence[6] are thereby disguised. It was for this reason that a great French economist of the last century denounced them as "a scheme for so plucking geese as to get the most feathers with the least squawking."[7]

---

5. "Taxes are either direct or indirect. A direct tax is one which is demanded from the very persons who, it is intended or desired, should pay it. Indirect taxes are those which are demanded from one person in the expectation and intention that he shall indemnify himself at the expense of another."—*John Stuart Mill's Prin. of Pol. Ec., book v, ch. iii, sec. 1.*

"Direct taxes are those which are levied on the very persons who it is intended or desired should pay them, and which they cannot put off upon others by raising the prices of the taxed article. . . Indirect taxes on the other hand are those which are levied on persons who expect to get back the amount of the tax by raising the price of the taxed article."—*Laughlin's Elements, par. 249.*

Taxes are direct "when the payment is made by the person who is intended to bear the sacrifice." Indirect taxes are recovered from final purchasers.—*Jevons's Primer, sec. 96.*

"Indirect taxes are so called because they are not paid into the treasury by the person who really bears the burden. The payer adds the amount of the tax to the price of the commodity taxed, and thus the taxation is concealed under the increased price of some article of luxury or convenience."—*Thompson's Pol. Ec., sec. 175.*

6. Jevons defines the incidence of a tax as "the manner in which it falls upon different classes of the population."—*Jevons's Primer, sec. 96.*

Sometimes called "repercussion," and refers "to the real as opposed to the nominal payment of taxes."—*Ely's Taxation, p. 64.*

7. Though his language was blunt, the sentiment does not essentially differ from that of "statesmen" of our day who meet all the moral and economic objections to indirect taxation with the one reply that the people would not consent to pay enough for the support of government if public revenues were collected from them directly.

Indirect taxation costs the real tax-payers much more than the government receives, partly because the middlemen through whose hands taxed commodities pass are able to exact compound profits upon the tax,[8] This means nothing but that the people are actually hoodwinked by indirect taxation into sustaining a government that they would not support if they knew it was maintained at their expense ; and instead of being a reason for continuing indirect taxation, would, if true. be one of the strongest of reasons for abolishing it. It is consistent neither with the plainest principles of democracy nor the simplest conceptions of morality.

8. A tax upon shoes, paid in the first instance by shoe manufacturers, enters into manufacturers' prices, and, together with the usual rate of profit upon that amount of investment, is recovered from wholesalers. The tax and the manufacturers' profit upon it then constitute part of the wholesale price and are collected from retailers. The retailers in turn collect the tax with all intermediate profits upon it, together with their usual rate of profit upon the whole, from final purchasers—the consumers of shoes. Thus what appears on the surface to be a tax upon shoe manufacturers proves upon examination to be an indirect tax upon shoe consumers, who pay in an accumulation of profits upon the tax considerably more than the government receives.

The effect would be the same if a tax upon their leather output were imposed upon tanners. Tanners would add to the price of leather the amount of the tax, plus their usual rate of profit upon a like investment, and collect the whole, together with the cost of hides, of transportation, of tanning and of selling, from shoe manufacturers, who would collect with their profit from retailers, who would collect with their profit from shoe consumers. The principle applies also when taxes are levied upon the stock or the sales of merchants, or the money or credits of bankers ; merchants add the tax with the usual profit to the prices of their goods, and bankers add it to their interest and discounts.

For example, a tax of $100,000 upon the output of manufacturers or importers would, at 10 per cent. as the manufacturing profit, cost wholesalers $110,000 ; at a profit of 10 per cent. to wholesalers it would cost retailers $121,000, and at 20 per cent. profit to retailers it would finally impose a tax burden of $145,200—being 45 per cent. more than the government would get. Upon most commodities the number of profits exceeds three, so that indirect taxes may frequently cost as much as 100 per cent., even when imposed only upon what are commercially known as finished goods ; when imposed upon materials also, the cost of collection might well run far above 200 per cent. in addition to the first cost of maintaining the machinery of taxation.

It must not be supposed, however, that the recovery of indirect taxes from the ultimate consumers of taxed goods is arbitrary. When shoe manufacturers, or tanners, or merchants add taxes to prices, or bankers add them to interest, it is not because they might do otherwise. but choose to do this ; it is because the exigencies of trade compel them. Manufacturers, merchants, and other tradesmen who carry on competitive businesses must on the average sell their goods at cost plus the ordinary rate of profit, or go out of business. It follows that any increase in cost of production tends to increase the price of products. Now, a tax upon the output of business men, which they must pay as a condition of doing their business, is as truly part of the cost of their output as is the price of the materials they buy or the wages of the men they hire. Therefore, such a tax upon business men tends to increase the price of their products. And this tendency is more or less marked as the tax is more or less great and competition more or less keen.

and partly on account of extraordinary expenses of original collection;⁹ it favors corruption in government by concealing from the people the fact that they contribute to the support of government; and it tends, by obstructing production, to crush legitimate industry and establish monopolies.¹⁰ The questions it raises are of vastly more concern than is indicated by the sum total of public expenditures.

Whoever calmly reflects and candidly decides upon the merits of indirect taxation must reject it in all its forms. But to do that is to make a great stride toward accepting the single tax. For the single tax is a form of direct taxation; it cannot be shifted."

It is true that a moderate tax upon monopolized products, such as trade-mark goods, proprietary medicines, patented articles and copyright publications is not necessarily shifted to consumers. The monopoly manufacturer whose prices are not checked by cost of production, and are therefore as a rule higher than competitive prices would be, may find it more profitable to bear the burden of a tax that leaves him some profit, thereby preserving his entire custom, than to drive off part of his custom by adding the tax to his usual prices. This is true also of a moderate import tax to the extent that it falls upon goods that are more cheaply transported from the place of production to a foreign market where the import tax is imposed than to a home market where the goods would be free of such a tax—products, for instance, of a farm in Canada near to a New York town, but far away from any Canadian town. If the tax be less than the difference in the cost of transportation the producer will bear the burden of it; otherwise he will not. The ultimate effect would be a reduction in the value of the Canadian land. Examples which may be cited in opposition to the principle that import taxes are indirect, will upon examination prove to be of the character here described. Business cannot be carried on at a loss—not for long.

9. " To collect taxes, to prevent and punish evasions, to check and countercheck revenues drawn from so many distinct sources, now make up probably three-fourths, perhaps seven-eighths, of the business of government outside of the preservation of order, the maintenance of the military arm, and the administration of justice."— *Progress and Poverty*, book iv, ch. v.

10. For a brief and thorough exposition of indirect taxation read George's " Protection or Free Trade," ch. viii, on " Tariffs for Revenue."

11. This is usually a stumbling block to those who, without much experience in economic thought, consider the single tax for the first time. As soon as they grasp the idea that taxes upon commodities shift to consumers they jump to the conclusion that similarly taxes upon land values would shift to the users. But this is a mistake, and the explanation is simple. Taxes upon what men produce make production more difficult and so tend toward scarcity in the supply, which stimulates prices; but taxes upon land, provided the taxes be levied in proportion to value, tend toward plenty in the supply (meaning market supply of course), because they make it more difficult to hold valuable land idle, and so depress prices.

2. THE TWO KINDS OF DIRECT TAXATION.

Direct taxes fall into two general classes: (1) Taxes that are levied upon men in proportion to their *ability to pay*, and (2) taxes that are levied in proportion to the *benefits received* by the tax-payer from the public. Income taxes are the principal ones of the first class, though probate and inheritance taxes would rank high. The single tax is the only important one of the second class.

There should be no difficulty in choosing between the two. To tax in proportion to ability to pay, re-

"A tax on rent falls wholly on the landlord. There are no means by which he can shift the burden upon any one else. . . . A tax on rent, therefore, has no effect other than its obvious one. It merely takes so much from the landlord and transfers it to the state."—*John Stuart Mill's Prin. of Pol. Ec., book v, ch. iii, sec.* 1.

"A tax laid upon rent is borne solely by the owner of land."—*Bascom's Tr., p.* 159.

"Taxes which are levied on land . . . really fall on the owner of the land."—*Mrs. Fawcett's Pol. Ec. for Beginners, pp.* 209, 210.

"A land tax levied in proportion to the rent of land, and varying with every variation of rents, . . . will fall wholly on the landlords."—*Walker's Pol. Ec., ed. of* 1887, *p.* 413, *quoting Ricardo.*

"The power of transferring a tax from the person who actually pays it to some other person varies with the object taxed. A tax on rents cannot be transferred. A tax on commodities is always transferred to the consumer."—*Thorold Rogers's Pol. Ec., ch. xxi, 2d ed., p.* 285.

"Though the landlord is in all cases the real contributor, the tax is commonly advanced by the tenant, to whom the landlord is obliged to allow it in payment of the rent."—*Adam Smith's Wealth of Nations, book v, ch. ii, part ii, art. i.*

"The way taxes raise prices is by increasing the cost of production and checking supply. But land is not a thing of human production, and taxes upon rent cannot check supply. Therefore, though a tax upon rent compels land-owners to pay more, it gives them no power to obtain more for the use of their land, as it in no way tends to reduce the supply of land. On the contrary, by compelling those who hold land on speculation to sell or let for what they can get, a tax on land values tends to increase the competition between owners, and thus to reduce the price of land."—*Progress and Poverty, book viii, ch. iii, subd. i.*

Sometimes this point is raised as a question of shifting the tax in higher rent to the tenant, and at others as a question of shifting it to the consumers of goods in higher prices. The principle is the same. Merchants cannot charge higher prices for goods than their competitors do, merely because they pay higher ground rents. A country storekeeper whose business lot is worth but a few dollars charges as much for sugar, probably more, than a city grocer whose lot is worth thousands. Quality for quality and quantity for quantity, goods sell for about the same price everywhere. Differences in price are altogether in favor of places where land has a high value.

gardless of benefits received, is in accord with no principle of just government; it is a device of piracy. The single tax, therefore, as the only important tax in proportion to benefits, is the ideal tax.

But here we encounter two plausible objections. One arises from the mistaken but common notion that men are not taxed in proportion to benefits unless they pay taxes upon every kind of property they own that comes under the protection of government; the other is founded in the assumption that it is impossible to measure the value of the public benefits that each

---

This is due to the fact that the cost of getting goods to places of low land value, distant villages for example, is greater than to centers, which are places of high land value. Sometimes it is true that prices for some things are higher where land values are high. Tiffany's goods, for instance, may be more expensive than goods of the same quality at a store on a less expensive site. But that is not due to the higher land value; it is because the dealer has a reputation for technical knowledge and honesty (or has become a fad among rich people), for which his customers are willing to pay whether his store is on a high priced lot or a low priced one.

Though land value has no effect upon the price of goods, it is easier to sell goods in some locations than in others. Therefore, though the price and the profit of each sale be the same, or even less, in good locations than in poorer ones, aggregate receipts and aggregate profits are much greater at the good location. And it is out of this aggregate, and not out of each profit, that rent is paid. For example: A cigar store on a thoroughfare supplies a certain quality of cigar for fifteen cents. On a side street the same quality of cigar can be bought no cheaper. Indeed, the cigars there are likely to be poorer, and therefore really dearer. Yet ground rent on the thoroughfare is very high compared with ground rent on the side street. How, then, can the first dealer, he who pays the high ground rent, afford to sell as good or better cigars for fifteen cents than his competitor of the low priced location? Simply because he is able to make so many more sales with a given outlay of labor and capital in a given time that his aggregate profit is greater. This is due to the advantage of his location. And for that advantage he pays a premium in higher ground rent. But that premium is not charged to smokers; the competing dealer of the side street protects them. It represents the greater ease, the lower cost, of doing a given volume of business upon the site for which it is paid; and if the state should take any of it, even the whole of it, in taxation, the loss would be finally borne by the owner of the advantage which attaches to that site—by the landlord. Any attempt to shift it to tenant or buyer would be promptly checked by the competition of neighboring but cheaper land.

"A land-tax, levied in proportion to the rent of land, and varying with every variation of rent, is in effect a tax on rent; and as such a tax will not apply to that land which yields no rent, nor to the produce of that capital which is employed on the land with a view to profit merely, and which never pays rent; it will not in any way affect the price of raw produce, but will fall wholly on the landlords."—*McCulloch's Ricardo* (3d ed.), p. 107.

individual enjoys. Though the first of these objections ostensibly accepts the doctrine of taxation according to benefits,[12] yet, as it leads to attempts at taxation in proportion to wealth, it, like the other, is really a plea for the piratical doctrine of taxation according to ability to pay. The two objections stand or fall together.

Let it once be perceived that the value of the service which government renders to each individual would be justly measured by the single tax, and neither objection would any longer have weight. We should then no more think of taxing people in proportion to their wealth or ability to pay, regardless of the benefits they receive from government, than an honest merchant would think of charging his customers in proportion to their wealth or ability to pay, regardless of the value of the goods they bought of him.[13]

---

12. It is often said, for instance, by its advocates, that house owners should in justice contribute to the support of the fire departments that protect them; and it is even gravely argued that houses are more appropriate subjects of taxation than land, because they need protection, whereas land needs none. Read note 8.

13. Following is an interesting computation of the cost and loss to the city of Boston of the present mixed system of taxation as compared with the single tax. The computation was made by James R. Carret, Esq., the leading conveyancer of Boston:

Valuation of Boston, May 1, 1892.

Land	$399,170,175
Buildings	281,109,700
Total assessed value of real estate	$680,279,875
Assessed value of personal estate	213,695,829
	$893,975,704

Rate of taxation, $12.90 per $1000.

Total tax levy, May 1, 1892 .... $11,805,036

Amount of taxes levied in respect of the different subjects of taxation and percentages of the same:

		Per cent.
Land	$5,149,295	43 63/100
Buildings	3,626,315	30 72/100
Personal estate	2,756,676	23 35/100
Polls	272,750	2 30/100
	$11,805,036	100

But to ascertain the total cost to the people of Boston of the present system of taxation for the taxable year, beginning May 1, 1892, there should be added to the

3. THE SINGLE TAX FALLS IN PROPOR ́ TO BENEFITS.

To perceive that the single tax would justly measure the value of government service we have only to realize that the mass of individuals everywhere and now, in paying for the land they use, actually pay for government service in proportion to what they receive. He who would enjoy the benefits of a government must use land within its jurisdiction. He cannot carry land from where government is poor to where it is good; neither can he carry it from where the benefits of good government are few or enjoyed with difficulty to where

taxes assessed upon them what it cost them to pay the owners of the land of Boston for the use of the land, being the net ground rent, which I estimate at four per cent. on the land value.

Total tax levy, May 1, 1892	$11,805,036
Net ground rent, four per cent. on the land value ($399,170,175)	15,966,807
Total cost of the present system to the people of Boston for that year	$27,771,843

To contrast this with what the single tax system would have cost the people of Boston for that year, take the gross ground rent, found by adding to the net ground rent the taxation on land values for that year, being $12.90 per $1000, or $1\frac{29}{100}$ per cent. added to 4 per cent., = $5\frac{29}{100}$ per cent.

Total cost of present system as above	$27,771,843
Single tax, or gross ground rent, $5\frac{29}{100}$ per cent. on $399,170,175	21,116,102
Excess of cost of present system, which is the sum of taxes in respect of buildings, personal property, and polls	$6,655,741

But the present system not only costs the people more than the single tax would, but produces less revenue:

Proceeds of single tax	$21,116,102
Present tax levy	11,805,036
Loss to public treasury by present system	$9,311,066

This, however, is not a complete contrast between the present system and the single tax, for large amounts of real estate are exempt from taxation, being held by the United States, the Commonwealth, by the city itself, by religious societies and corporations, and by charitable, literary, and scientific institutions. The total amount of the value of land so held as returned by the assessors for the year 1892 is $60,626,171.

Reasons can be given why all lands within the city should be assessed for taxation to secure a just distribution of the public burdens, which I cannot take the space to enter into here. There is good reason to believe also that lands in the city of Boston are assessed to quite an appreciable extent below their fair market value. As an indication of this see an editorial in the Boston *Daily Advertiser* for October 3, 1893, under the title, "Their Own Figures."

The vacant lands, marsh lands, and flats in Boston were valued by the assessors in 1892 (page 3 of their annual report) at $52,712,600. I believe that this represents not more than fifty per cent. of their true market value.

Taking this and the undervaluation of improved property and the exemptions above mentioned into consideration, I think $500,000,000 to be a fair estimate of the land values of Boston. Making this the basis of contrast, we have:

Proceeds of single tax $5\frac{29}{100}$ per cent. on $500,000,000	$26,450,000
Present tax levy	11,805,036
Loss to public treasury by present system	$14,644,974

the⸺ ⸺e many and fully enjoyed. He must rent or bu⸺ ⸺nd where the benefits of government are available, or forego them. And unless he buys or rents where they are greatest and most available he must forego them in degree. Consequently, if he would work or live where the benefits of government are available, and does not already own land there, he will be compelled to rent or buy at a valuation which, other things being equal, will depend upon the value of the government service that the site he selects enables him to enjoy." Thus does he pay for the service of govern-

14. Land values are lower in all countries of poor government than in any country of better government, other things being equal. They are lower in cities of poor government, other things being equal, than in cities of better government. Land values are lower, for example, in Juarez, on the Mexican side of the Rio Grande, where government is bad, than in El Paso, the neighboring city on the American side, where government is better. They are lower in the same city under bad government than under improved government. When Seth Low, after a reform campaign, was elected mayor of Brooklyn, N. Y., rents advanced before he took the oath of office, upon the bare expectation that he would eradicate municipal abuses. Let the city authorities anywhere pave a street, put water through it and sewer it, or do any of these things, and lots in the neighborhood rise in value. Everywhere that the " good roads " agitation of wheelmen has borne fruit in better highways, the value of adjacent land has increased. Instances of this effect as results of public improvements might be collected in abundance. Every man must be able to recall some within his own experience.

And it is perfectly reasonable that it should be so. Land and not other property must rise in value with desired improvements in government, because, while any tendency on the part of other kinds of property to rise in value is checked by greater production, land can not be reproduced.

Imagine an utterly lawless place, where life and property are constantly threatened by desperadoes. He must be either a very bold man or a very avaricious one who will build a store in such a community and stock it with goods; but suppose such a man should appear. His store costs him more than the same building would cost in a civilized community; mechanics are not plentiful in such a place, and materials are hard to get. The building is finally erected, however, and stocked. And now what about this merchant's prices for goods? Competition is weak, because there are few men who will take the chances he has taken, and he charges all that his customers will pay. A hundred per cent., five hundred per cent., perhaps one or two thousand per cent. profit rewards him for his pains and risk. His goods are dear, enormously dear—dear enough to satisfy the most contemptuous enemy of cheapness; and if any one should wish to buy his store that would be dear too, for the difficulties in the way of building continue. *But land is cheap!* This is the type of community in which may be found that land, so often mentioned and so seldom seen, which " the owners actually can't give away, you know ! "

ment in proportion to its value to him. But he does not pay the public which provides the service; he is required to pay land-owners.

Now, the economic principle pursuant to which land-owners are thus able to charge their fellow-citizens for the common benefits of their common government points to the true method of taxation. With the exception of such other monopoly property as is analogous to land titles, and which in the purview of the single tax is included with land for purposes of taxation,[14] land is the only kind of property that is increased in value by government; and the increase of value is in proportion, other influences aside, to the public service which its possession secures to the occupant. Therefore, by taxing land in proportion to its value, and exempting all other property, kindred monopolies excepted—that is to say, by adopting the single tax—we should be levying taxes according to benefits.[16]

And in no sense would this be class taxation. Indeed, the cry of class taxation is a rather impudent

---

But suppose that government improves. An efficient administration of justice rids the place of desperadoes, and life and property are safe. What about prices then? It would no longer require a bold or desperately avaricious man to engage in selling goods in that community, and competition would set in. High profits would soon come down. Goods would be cheap—as cheap as anywhere in the world, the cost of transportation considered. Builders and building materials could be had without difficulty, and stores would be cheap, too. *But land would be dear!* Improvement in government increases the value of that, and of that alone.

15. Railroad franchises, for example, are not usually thought of as land titles, but that is what they are. By an act of sovereign authority they confer rights of control for transportation purposes over narrow strips of land between terminals and along trading points. The value of this right of way is a land value.

16. Each occupant would pay to his landlord the value of the public benefits in the way of highways, schools, courts, police and fire protection, etc., that his site enabled him to enjoy. The landlord would pay a tax proportioned to the pecuniary benefits conferred upon him by the public in raising and maintaining the value of his holding. And if occupant and owner were the same, he would pay directly according to the value of his land for all the public benefits he enjoyed, both intangible and pecuniary.

one for owners of valuable land to raise against the single tax, when it is considered that under existing systems of taxation they are exempt." Even the poorest and the most degraded classes in the community, besides paying land-owners for such public benefits as come their way, are compelled by indirect taxation to contribute to the support of government. But land-owners as a class go free. They enjoy the protection of the courts, and of police and fire departments, and they have the use of schools and the benefit of highways and other public improvements, all in common with the most favored, and upon the same specific terms ; yet, though they go through the form of paying taxes, and if their holdings are of considerable value pose as "*the* tax-payers" on all important occasions, they, in effect, and considered as a class, pay no taxes, because government, by increasing the value of their land, enables them to recover back in higher rents and higher prices more than their taxes amount to. Enjoying the same intangible benefits of government that others do, many of them as individuals and all of them as a class receive in addition a tangible

---

17. While the land-owners of the City of Washington were paying something less than two per cent. annually in taxes, a Congressional Committee (*Report of the Select Committee to Investigate Tax Assessments in the District of Columbia, composed of Messrs. Johnson, of Ohio, Chairman ; Wadsworth, of New York, and Washington, of Tennessee. Made to the House of Representatives, May 24, 1892. Report No.* 1469), brought out the fact that the value of their land had been increasing at a minimum rate of ten per cent. per annum. The Washington land-owners as a class thus appear to have received back in higher land values, actually and potentially, about ten dollars for every two dollars that as land-owners they paid in taxes. If any one supposes that this condition is peculiar to Washington let him make similar estimates for any progressive locality, and see if the land-owners there are not favored in like manner.

But the point is not dependent upon increase in the capitalized value of land. If the land yields or will yield to its owner an income in the nature of actual or potential ground rent, then to the extent that this actual or possible income is dependent upon government the landlord is in effect exempt from taxation. No matter what tax he pays on account of his ownership of land, the public gives it back to him to that extent.

pecuniary benefit which government confers upon no other property-owners. The value of their property is enhanced in proportion to the benefits of government which its occupants enjoy. To tax them alone, therefore, is not to discriminate against them; it is to charge them for what they get.[18]

[18]. Take for illustration two towns, one of excellent government and the other of inefficient government, but in all other respects alike. Suppose you are hunting for a place of residence and find a suitable site in the town of good government. For simplicity of illustration let us suppose that the land there is not sold outright but is let upon ground rent. You meet the owner of the lot you have selected and ask him his terms. He replies:

"Two hundred and fifty dollars a year."

"Two hundred and fifty dollars a year!" you exclaim. "Why, I can get just as good a site in that other town for a hundred dollars a year."

"Certainly you can," he will say. "But if you build a house there and it catches fire it will burn down; they have no fire department. If you go out after dark you will be 'held up' and robbed; they have no police force. If you ride out in the spring, your carriage will stick in the mud up to the hubs, and if you walk you may break your legs and will be lucky if you don't break your neck; they have no street pavements and their sidewalks are dangerously out of repair. When the moon doesn't shine the streets are in darkness, for they have no street lights. The water you need for your house you must get from a well; there is no water supply there. Now in our town it is different. We have a splendid fire department, and the best police force in the world. Our streets are macadamized, and lighted with electricity; our sidewalks are always in first class repair; we have a water system that equals that of New York; and in every way the public benefits in this town are unsurpassed. It is the best governed town in all this region. Isn't it worth a hundred and fifty dollars a year more for a building site here than over in that poorly governed town?"

You recognize the advantages and agree to the terms.

But when your house is built and the assessor visits you officially, what would be the conversation if your sense of the fitness of things were not warped by familiarity with false systems of taxation? Would it not be something like what follows?

"How much do you regard this house as worth?" asks the assessor.

"What is that to you?" you inquire.

"I am the town assessor and am about to appraise your property for taxation."

"Am I to be taxed by this town? What for?"

"What for?" echoes the assessor in surprise. "What for? Is not your house protected from fire by our magnificent fire department. Are not you protected from robbery by the best police force in the world? Do not you have the use of macadamized pavements, and good sidewalks, and electric street lights, and a first class water supply? Don't you suppose these things cost something? And don't you think you ought to pay your share?"

"Yes," you answer, with more or less calmness; "I do have the benefit of these things, and I do think that I ought to pay my share toward supporting them. But I have already paid my share for this year. I have paid it to the owner of this lot. He charges me two hundred and fifty dollars a year—one hundred and fifty dollars more than I should pay or he could get but for those very benefits. *He* has collected my

4. CONFORMITY TO GENERAL PRINCIPLES OF TAXATION.

The single tax conforms most closely to the essential principles of Adam Smith's four classical maxims, which are stated best by Henry George[19] as follows:

The best tax by which public revenues can be raised is evidently that which will closest conform to the following conditions:

1. That it bear as lightly as possible upon production—so as least to check the increase of the general fund from which taxes must be paid and the community maintained.[20]

2. That it be easily and cheaply collected, and fall as directly as may be upon the ultimate payers—so as to take from the people as little as possible in addition to what it yields the government.[21]

3. That it be certain—so as to give the least opportunity for tyranny or corruption on the part of officials, and the least temptation to law-breaking and evasion on the part of the tax-payers.[22]

4. That it bear equally—so as to give no citizen an advantage or put any at a disadvantage, as compared with others.[23]

---

share of this year's expense of maintaining town improvements; you go and collect from him. If you do not, but insist upon collecting from me, I shall be paying twice for these things, once to him and once to you; and he won't be paying at all, but will be making money out of them, although he derives the same benefits from them in all other respects that I do."

19. "Progress and Poverty," book viii, ch. iii.

20. This is the second part of Adam Smith's fourth maxim. He states it as follows: "Every tax ought to be so contrived as both to take out and to keep out of the pockets of the people as little as possible over and above what it brings into the public treasury of the state. A tax may either take out or keep out of the pockets of the people a great deal more than it brings into the public treasury in the four following ways: . . . Secondly, it may obstruct the industry of the people, and discourage them from applying to certain branches of business which might give maintenance and employment to great multitudes. While it obliges the people to pay, it may thus diminish or perhaps destroy some of the funds which might enable them more easily to do so."

21. This is the first part of Adam Smith's fourth maxim, in which he condemns a tax that takes out of the pockets of the people more than it brings into the public treasury.

22. This is Adam Smith's second maxim. He states it as follows: "The tax which each individual is bound to pay ought to be certain and not arbitrary. The time of payment, the manner of payment, the quantity to be paid, ought all to be clear and plain to the contributor and to every other person. Where it is otherwise, every person subject to the tax is put more or less in the power of the tax gatherer."

23. This is Adam Smith's first maxim. He states it as follows: "The subjects of every state ought to contribute towards the support of the government as nearly as

a. *Interference with Production.*

Indirect taxes tend to check production and cause scarcity by obstructing the processes of production. They fall upon men *as* they work, *as* they do business, *as* they invest capital productively." But the single tax, which must be paid and be the same in amount regardless of whether the payer works or plays, of whether he invests his capital productively or wastes it, of whether he uses his land for the most productive purposes [25] or in lesser degree or not at all, removes all fiscal penalties from industry and thrift, and tends to

possible in proportion to their respective abilities, that is to say, in proportion to the revenue which they respectively enjoy under the protection of the state. The expense of government to the individuals of a great nation is like the expense of management to the joint tenants of a great estate, who are all obliged to contribute in proportion to their respective interests in the estate. In the observation or neglect of this maxim consists what is called the equality or inequality of taxation."

In changing this Mr. George says (" Progress and Poverty," book viii, ch. iii, subd. 4): "Adam Smith speaks of incomes as enjoyed 'under the protection of the state'; and this is the ground upon which the equal taxation of all species of property is commonly insisted upon—that it is equally protected by the state. The basis of this idea is evidently that the enjoyment of property is made possible by the state—that there is a value created and maintained by the community, which is justly called upon to meet community expenses. Now, of what values is this true ? Only of the value of land. This is a value that does not arise until a community is formed, and that, unlike other values, grows with the growth of the community. It only exists as the community exists. Scatter again the largest community, and land, now so valuable, would have no value at all. With every increase of population the value of land rises ; with every decrease it falls. This is true of nothing else save of things which, like the ownership of land, are in their nature monopolies."

Adam Smith's third maxim refers only to conveniency of payment, and gives countenance to indirect taxation, which is in conflict with the principle of his fourth maxim. Mr. George properly excludes it.

24. " Taxation which falls upon the processes of production interposes an artificial obstacle to the creation of wealth. Taxation which falls upon labor *as* it is exerted, wealth *as* it is used as capital, land *as* it is cultivated, will manifestly tend to discourage production much more powerfully than taxation to the same amount levied upon laborers whether they work or play, upon wealth whether used productively or unproductively, or upon land whether cultivated or left waste."—*Progress and Poverty*, *book viii, ch. iii, subd.* 1.

25. It is common, besides taxing improvements as fast as they are made, to levy higher taxes upon land when put to its best use than when put to partial use or to no use at all. This is upon the theory that when his land is used the owner gets full income from it and can afford to pay high taxes ; but that he gets little or no income when the land is out of use, and so cannot afford to pay much. It is an absurd but perfectly

leave production free. It therefore conforms more closely than indirect taxation to the first maxim quoted above.

b. *Cheapness of Collection.*

Indirect taxes are passed along from first payers to final consumers through many exchanges, accumulating compound profits as they go, until they take enormous sums from the people in addition to what the government receives.[26] But the single tax takes nothing from the people in excess of the tax. It therefore conforms more closely than indirect taxation to the second maxim quoted above.

c. *Certainty.*

No other tax, direct or indirect, conforms so closely to the third maxim. "Land lies out of doors." It cannot be hidden; it cannot be "accidentally" over-

---

legitimate illustration of the pretentious doctrine of taxation according to ability to pay.

Examples are numerous. Improved building lots, and even those that are only plotted for improvement, are usually taxed more than contiguous unused and unplotted land which is equally in demand for building purposes and equally valuable. So coal land, iron land, oil land, and sugar land are as a rule taxed less as land when opened up for appropriate use than when lying idle or put to inferior uses, though the land value be the same. Any serious proposal to put land to its appropriate use is commonly regarded as a signal for increasing the tax upon it.

26. "All taxes upon things of unfixed quantity increase prices, and in the course of exchange are shifted from seller to buyer, increasing as they go. If we impose a tax on money loaned, as has been often attempted, the lender will charge the tax to the borrower, and the borrower must pay it or not obtain the loan. If the borrower uses it in his business, he in his turn must get back the tax from his customers, or his business becomes unprofitable. If we impose a tax upon buildings, the users of buildings must finally pay it, for the erection of buildings will cease until building rents become high enough to pay the regular profit and the tax besides. If we impose a tax upon manufactures or imported goods, the manufacturer or importer will charge it in a higher price to the jobber, the jobber to the retailer, and the retailer to the consumer. Now, the consumer, on whom the tax thus ultimately falls, must not only pay the amount of the tax, but also a profit on this amount to every one who has thus advanced it—for profit on the capital he has advanced in paying taxes is as much required by each dealer as profit on the capital he has advanced in paying for goods."—*Progress and Poverty, book viii, ch. iii, subd.* 2.

looked. Nor can its value be seriously misstated. Neither under-appraisement nor over-appraisement to any important degree is possible without the connivance of the whole community.[27] The land values of a neighborhood are matters of common knowledge. Any intelligent resident can justly appraise them, and every other intelligent resident can fairly test the appraisement. Therefore the tyranny, corruption, fraud, favoritism, and evasions that are so common in connection with the taxation of imports, manufactures, incomes, personal property, and buildings—the values of which, even when the object itself cannot be hidden, are so distinctly matters of minute special knowledge that only experts can fairly appraise them—would be out of the question if the single tax were substituted for existing fiscal methods.[28]

27. The under-appraisements so common at present, and alluded to in note 25, are possible because the community, ignorant of the just principles of taxation, does connive at them. Under-appraisements are not secret crimes on the part of assessors; they are distinctly recognized, but thoughtlessly disregarded when not actually insisted upon, by the people themselves. And this is due to the dishonest ideas of taxation that are taught. Let the vicious doctrine that people ought to pay taxes according to their ability give way to the honest principle that they should pay in proportion to the benefits they receive, which benefits, as we have already seen, are measured by the land values they own, and underappraisement of land would cease. No assessor can befool the community in respect of the value of the land within his jurisdiction.

And, with the cessation of general under-appraisement, favoritism in individual appraisements also would cease. General under-appraisement fosters unfair individual appraisements. If land were generally appraised at its full value, a particular unfair appraisement would stand out in such relief that the crime of the assessor would be exposed. But now if a man's land is appraised at a higher valuation than his neighbor's equally valuable land, and he complains of the unfairness, he is promptly and effectually silenced with a warning that his land is worth much more than it is appraised at, anyhow, and if he makes a fuss his appraisement will be increased. To complain further of the deficient taxation of his neighbor is to invite the imposition of a higher tax upon himself.

28. If you wish to test the merits in point of certainty of the single tax as compared with other taxes, go to a real estate agent in your community and, showing him a building lot upon the map, ask him its value. If he inquires about the improvements, instruct him to ignore them. He will be able at once to tell you what the lot is worth. And if you go to twenty other agents their estimates will not materially vary from his. Yet none of the agents will have left his office. Each will have inferred the value from the size and location of the lot.

d. *Equality.*

In respect of the fourth maxim the single tax bears more equally—that is to say, more justly—than any other tax. It is the only tax that falls upon the taxpayer in proportion to the pecuniary benefits he receives from the public;[29] and its tendency, accelerating with the increase of the tax, is to leave to every one the full fruit of his own productive enterprise and effort.[30]

But suppose when you show the map to the first agent you ask him the value of the land *and* its improvements. He will tell you that he cannot give an estimate until he examines the improvements. And if it is the highly improved property of a rich man he will engage building experts to assist him. Should you ask him to include the value of the contents of the buildings, he would need a corps of selected experts, including artists and liverymen, dealers in furniture and bric-à-brac, librarians and jewelers. Should you propose that he also include the value of the occupant's income, the agent would throw up his hands in despair.

If without the aid of an army of experts the agent should make an estimate of these miscellaneous values, and twenty others should do the same, their several estimates would be as wide apart as ignorant guesses usually are. And the richer the owner of the property the lower as a proportion would the guesses probably be.

Now turn the real estate agent into an assessor, and is it not plain that he would appraise land values with much greater certainty and cheapness than he could appraise the values of all kinds of property? With a plot map before him he might fairly make every appraisement without leaving his desk at the town hall.

And there would be no material difference if the property in question were a farm instead of a building lot. A competent farmer or business man in a farming community can, without leaving his own door-yard, appraise the value of the land of any farm there; whereas it would be impossible for him to value the improvements, stock, produce, etc., without at least inspecting them.

29. The benefits of government are not the only public benefits whose value attaches exclusively to land. Communal development from whatever cause produces the same effect. But as it is under the protection of government that land-owners are able to maintain ownership of land and through that to enjoy the pecuniary benefits of advancing social conditions, government confers upon them as a class not only the pecuniary benefits of good government, but also the pecuniary benefits of progress in general.

30. "Here are two men of equal incomes—that of the one derived from the exertion of his labor, that of the other from rent of land. Is it just that they should equally contribute to the expenses of the state? Evidently not. The income of the one represents wealth he creates and adds to the general wealth of the state; the income of the other represents merely wealth that he takes from the general stock, returning nothing."—*Progress and Poverty*, book *viii*, ch. *iii*, subd. 4.

III. THE SINGLE TAX AS A SOCIAL REFORM.

But the single tax is more than a revenue system. Great as are its merits in this respect, they are but incidental to its character as a social reform.[31] And that some social reform, which shall be simple in method but fundamental in character, is most urgently needed we have only to look about us to see.

Poverty is widespread and pitiable. This we know. Its general manifestations are so common that even good men look upon it as a providential provision for enabling the rich to drive camels through needles' eyes by exercising the modern virtue of organized giving.[32] Its occasional manifestations in recurring

---

31. There are two classes of single tax advocates. Those who advocate it as a reform in taxation alone, regardless of its effects upon social adjustments, are called "single tax men limited"; those who advocate it both as a reform in taxation and as the mode of securing equal rights to land, are called "single tax men unlimited."

32. Not all charity is contemptible. Those charitable people, who, knowing that individuals suffer, hasten to their relief, deserve the respect and affection they receive. That kind of charity is neighborliness; it is love. And perhaps in modern circumstances organization is necessary to make it effective. But organized charity as a cherished social institution is a different thing. It is not love, nor is it inspired by love; it is simply sanctified selfishness, at the bottom of which will be found the blasphemous notion that in the economy of God the poor are to be forever with us that the rich may gain heaven by alms-giving.

Suppose a hole in the sidewalk into which passers-by continually fall, breaking their arms, their legs, and sometimes their necks. We should respect charitable people who, without thought of themselves, went to the relief of the sufferers, binding the broken limbs of the living, and decently burying the dead. But what should we say of those who, when some one proposed to fill up the hole to prevent further suffering, should say, "Oh, you mustn't fill up that hole! Whatever in the world should we charitable people do to be saved if we had no broken legs and arms to bind, and no broken-necked people to bury?"

Of some kinds of charity it has been well said that they are "that form of self-righteousness which makes us give to others the things that already belong to them." They suggest the old nursery rhyme:

> "There was once a considerate crocodile,
> Which lay on a bank of the river Nile.
> And he swallowed a fish, with a face of woe,
> While his tears flowed fast to the stream below.
> 'I am mourning,' said he, 'the untimely fate
> Of the dear little fish which I just now ate.'"

Read Chapter viii of "Social Problems," by Henry George, entitled, "That We All Might be Rich."

periods of "hard times"[33] are like epidemics of a virulent disease, which excite even the most contented to ask if they may not be the next victims. Its spasms of violence threaten society with anarchy on the one hand, and, through panic-stricken efforts at restraint, with loss of liberty on the other. And it persists and deepens despite the continuous increase of wealth-producing power.[34]

33. Differences between "hard times" and "good times" are but differences in degrees of poverty and in the people who suffer from it. Times are always hard with the multitude. But the voice of the multitude is too weak to be heard at ordinary times through the ordinary trumpets of public opinion. They are not regarded nor do they regard themselves as people of any importance in the industrial world, so long as the general wheels of business revolve. It is only when poverty has eaten its way up through the various strata of struggling and pinching and squeezing and squirming humanity, and with its cancerous tentacles touched the superincumbent layers of manufacturing nabobs, merchant princes, railroad kings, great bankers and great land-owners that we hear any general complaint of "hard times."

34. "Could a man of the last century—a Franklin or a Priestley—have seen, in a vision of the future, the steamship taking the place of the sailing vessel, the railroad train of the wagon, the reaping machine of the scythe, the threshing machine of the flail; could he have heard the throb of the engines that in obedience to human will, and for the satisfaction of human desire, exert a power greater than that of all the men and all the beasts of burden of the earth combined; could he have seen the forest tree transformed into finished lumber—into doors, sashes, blinds, boxes or barrels, with hardly the touch of a human hand; the great workshops where boots and shoes are turned out by the case with less labor than the old-fashioned cobbler could have put on a sole; the factories where, under the eye of a girl, cotton becomes cloth faster than hundreds of stalwart weavers could have turned it out with their hand-looms; could he have seen steam hammers shaping mammoth shafts and mighty anchors, and delicate machinery making tiny watches; the diamond drill cutting through the heart of the rocks, and coal oil sparing the whale; could he have realized the enormous saving of labor resulting from improved facilities of exchange and communication—sheep killed in Australia eaten fresh in England, and the order given by the London banker in the afternoon executed in San Francisco in the morning of the same day; could he have conceived of the hundred thousand improvements which these only suggest, what would he have inferred as to the social condition of mankind?

"It would not have seemed like an inference; further than the vision went, it would have seemed as though he saw; and his heart would have leaped and his nerves would have thrilled, as one who from a height beholds just ahead of the thirst-stricken caravan the living gleam of rustling woods and the glint of laughing waters. Plainly, in the sight of the imagination, he would have beheld these new forces elevating society from its very foundations, lifting the very poorest above the possibility of want, exempting the very lowest from anxiety for the material needs of life... And out of these bounteous material conditions he would have seen arising, as necessary sequences, moral conditions realizing the golden age of which mankind have always dreamed... More or less vague or clear, these have been the hopes,

That much of our poverty is involuntary may be proved, if proof be necessary, by the magnitude of charitable work that aims to help only the "deserving poor"; and as to undeserving cases—the cases of voluntary poverty—who can say but that they, if not due to birth and training in the environs of degraded poverty,[35] are the despairing culminations of long-con-

these the dreams born of the improvements which give this wonderful century its pre-eminence. . . . It is true that disappointment has followed disappointment, and that discovery upon discovery, and invention after invention, have neither lessened the toil of those who most need respite, nor brought plenty to the poor. But there have been so many things to which it seemed this failure could be laid, that up to our time the new faith has hardly weakened. . . Now, however, we are coming into collision with facts which there can be no mistaking. . . And, unpleasant as it may be to admit it, it is at last becoming evident that the enormous increase in productive power which has marked the present century and is still going on with accelerating ratio, has no tendency to extirpate poverty or to lighten the burdens of those compelled to toil. It simply widens the gulf between Dives and Lazarus, and makes the struggle for existence more intense. The march of invention has clothed mankind with powers of which a century ago the boldest imagination could not have dreamed. But in factories where labor saving machinery has reached its most wonderful development little children are at work ; wherever the new forces are anything like fully utilized large classes are maintained by charity or live on the verge of recourse to it ; amid the greatest accumulations of wealth, men die of starvation, and puny infants suckle dry breasts ; while everywhere the greed of gain, the worship of wealth, shows the force of the fear of want."—*Progress and Poverty, Introduction.*

35. The leader of one of the labor strikes of the early eighties, a hard-working, respectable, and self-respecting man, told me that the deprivations which he himself suffered as a workingman were as nothing compared with the fear for the future of his children that he felt whenever he thought of the repulsive surroundings, physical and moral, in which, owing to his poverty, he was compelled to bring them up.

Professor Francis Wayland, Dean of the Yale law school, wrote in the *Charities' Review* for March, 1893: "Under our eyes and within our reach children are being reared from infancy amid surroundings containing every conceivable element of degradation, depravity and vice. Why, then, should we be surprised that we are surrounded by a horde of juvenile delinquents, that the police reports in our cities teem with the exploits of precocious little villains, that reform schools are crowded with hopelessly abandoned young offenders? How could it be otherwise? What else could be expected from such antecedents, from such ever-present examples of flagrant vice? Short of a miracle, how could any child escape the moral contagion of such an environment? How could he retain a single vestige of virtue, a single honest impulse, a single shred of respect for the rights of others, after passing through such an ordeal of iniquity? What is there left on which to build up a better character?"

In the *Arena* of July, 1893, Helen Campbell says : " It would seem at times as if the workshop meant only a form of preparation for the hospital, the workhouse and

tinued struggles for respectable independence?[36] How can we know that they are not essentially like the rest —involuntary and deserving? It is a profound disthe prison, since the workers therein become inoculated with trade diseases, mutilated by trade appliances, and corrupted by trade associates till no healthy fiber, mental, moral, or physical, remains."

Such testimony is abundant. But no further citation is necessary to arouse the conscience of the merciful and the just, and any amount of proof would not affect those self-satisfied mortals whom Kipling describes when he says that "there are men who, when their own front doors are closed, will swear that the whole world's warm."

36. Some years ago a gentleman, now well and favorably known in New York public life, told me of a ragged tramp whom he had brought, more to gratify a whim perhaps than in any spirit of philanthropy, from a neighboring camp of tramps to his house for breakfast. After breakfast the host asked his guest, in the course of conversation, why he lived the life of a tramp. This in substance was the tramp's reply:

"I am a mechanic and used to be a good one, though not so exceptionally good as to be safe from the competition of the great class of average workers. I had a family—a wife and two children. In the hard times of the seventies I lost my job. For a while we lived upon our little savings; but sickness came and our savings were used up. My wife and children died. Everything was gone but self-respect. Then I traveled, looking for work which could not be had at home. I traveled afoot; I could afford no other way. For days I hunted for work, begging food and sleeping in barns or under trees; but no work could I get. Once or twice I was arrested as a vagrant. Then I fell in with a party of tramps and with them drifted into the city. Winter came on. I still had a desire to regain my old place as a self-respecting man, but work was scarce and nothing that I could do could I find to do, except some little job now and then which was given to me as pennies are given to beggars. I slept mostly in station houses. Part of the time I was undergoing sentence for vagrancy. In the spring I tramped again. But now I did not hunt for work. My self-respect was gone so completely that I had no ambition to regain it. I was a loafer and a jailbird. I had no family to support, and I had found that, barring the question of self-respect, I was about as well off as were average workmen. After years of tramping this opinion is unchanged. I am always sure of enough to eat and a place to sleep in— not very good often, but good enough. I should not be sure of that if I were a workingman. I might lose my job and go hungry rather than beg. I might be unable to pay my rent and so be turned upon the street. I might marry again and have a family which would be condemned to the hard life of the average workingman's family. And as for society, why, I have society. Tramps are good fellows—sociable fellows, bright fellows many of them. Life as a tramp is not half bad when you compare it with the workingman's life, leaving out the question of self-respect, of course. You must leave that out. No man can be a tramp for good until he loses that. But a period of hard times makes many a chap lose it. And as I have lost it I would rather be a tramp than a workingman. I have tried both. By the way, Mr.——, this is a very good cigar—this brand of yours. I seldom smoke much better cigars."

The facts in detail of this man's story may have been false; they probably were. But so were the facts in detail of Bunyan's "Pilgrim's Progress." There is, however, a distinction between *fact* and *truth*, and no matter how false the man's facts may have been, his story, like Bunyan's, was essentially true. Much of the poverty that

tinction that a clever writer of fiction[37] makes when he speaks of "the hopeful and the hopeless poor." There is, indeed, little difference between voluntary and involuntary poverty, between the "deserving" and the "undeserving" poor, except that the "deserving" still have hope, while from the "undeserving" all hope, if they ever knew any, has gone.

But it is not alone to objects of charity that the question of poverty calls our attention. There is a keener poverty, which pinches and goes hungry, but is beyond the reach of charity because it never complains. And back of all and over all is fear of poverty, which chills the best instincts of men of every social grade, from recipients of out-door relief who dread the poorhouse, to millionaires who dread the possibility of poverty for their children if not for themselves.[38]

It is poverty and fear of poverty that prompt men of honest instincts to steal, to bribe, to take bribes, to oppress, either under color of law or against law, and—what is worse than all, because it is not merely a depraved act, but a course of conduct that implies a state of depravity—to enlist their talents in crusades against

upon the surface seems to be voluntary and undeserving comes from a growing feeling among those who work hardest that, as Cowper describes it, they are

"Letting down buckets into empty wells,
And growing old with drawing nothing up."

At Victoria, B. C., in the spring of 1894, I witnessed a canoe race in which there were two contestants and but one prize. Long before the winner had reached the goal his adversary, who found himself far behind, turned his canoe toward the shore and dropped out of the race. Was it because he was too lazy to paddle? Not at all. It was because he realized the hopelessness of the effort.

37. H. C. Bunner, editor of *Puck*.

38. A well known millionaire is quoted as saying: "I would rather leave my children penniless in a world in which they could at all times obtain employment for wages equal to the value of their work as measured by the work of others, than to leave them millions of dollars in a world like this, where if they lose their inheritance they may have no chance of earning a decent living."

their convictions." Our civilization cannot long resist such enemies as poverty and fear of poverty breed; to intelligent observers it already seems to yield."

39. " From whence springs this lust for gain, to gratify which men tread everything pure and noble under their feet; to which they sacrifice all the higher possibilities of life; which converts civility into a hollow pretense, patriotism into a sham, and religion into hypocrisy; which makes so much of civilized existence an Ishmaelitish warfare, of which the weapons are cunning and fraud? Does it not spring from the existence of want? Carlyle somewhere says that poverty is the hell of which the modern Englishman is most afraid. And he is right. Poverty is the open-mouthed, relentless hell which yawns beneath civilized society. And it is hell enough. The Vedas declare no truer thing than when the wise crow Bushanda tells the eagle bearer of Vishnu that the keenest pain is in poverty. For poverty is not merely deprivation; it means shame, degradation; the searing of the most sensitive parts of our moral and mental nature as with hot irons; the denial of the strongest impulses and the sweetest affections; the wrenching of the most vital nerves. You love your wife, you love your children; but would it not be easier to see them die than to see them reduced to the pinch of want in which large classes in every civilized community live? . . . From this hell of poverty it is but natural that men should make every effort to escape. With the impulse to self-preservation and self-gratification combine nobler feelings, and love as well as fear urges in the struggle. Many a man does a mean thing, a dishonest thing, a greedy and grasping and unjust thing, in the effort to place above want, or the fear of want, mother or wife or children."—*Progress and Poverty, book ix, ch. iv.*

40. " There is just now a disposition to scoff at any implication that we are not in all respects progressing. . . Yet it is evident that there have been times of decline, just as there have been times of advance; and it is further evident that these epochs of decline could not at first have been generally recognized.

" He would have been a rash man who, when Augustus was changing the Rome of brick to the Rome of marble, when wealth was augmenting and magnificence increasing, when victorious legions were extending the frontier, when manners were becoming more refined, language more polished, and literature rising to higher splendors—he would have been a rash man who then would have said that Rome was entering her decline. Yet such was the case.

" And whoever will look may see that though our civilization is apparently advancing with greater rapidity than ever, the same cause which turned Roman progress into retrogression is operating now.

" What has destroyed every previous civilization has been the tendency to the unequal distribution of wealth and power. This same tendency, operating with increasing force, is observable in our civilization to-day, showing itself in every progressive community, and with greater intensity the more progressive the community. . . . The conditions of social progress, as we have traced the law, are association and equality. The general tendency of modern development, since the time when we can first discern the gleams of civilization in the darkness which followed the fall of the Western Empire, has been toward political and legal equality. . . This tendency has reached its full expression in the American Republic, where political and legal rights are absolutely equal. . . It is the prevailing tendency, and how soon Europe will be completely republican is only a matter of time, or rather of accident. The United States are, therefore, in this respect, the most advanced of all the great nations in a direction in which all are advancing, and in the United States we see just how much this tendency to personal and political freedom can of itself accomplish. . . It is now . . .

But how is the development of these social enemies to be arrested? Only by tracing poverty to its cause, and, having found the cause, deliberately removing it. Poverty cannot be traced to its cause, however, without serious thought; not mere reading and school

evident that political equality, co-existing with an increasing tendency to the unequal distribution of wealth, must ultimately beget either the despotism of organized tyranny or the worse despotism of anarchy.

"To turn a republican government into a despotism the basest and most brutal, it is not necessary to formally change its constitution or abandon popular elections. It was centuries after Cæsar before the absolute master of the Roman world pretended to rule other than by authority of a Senate that trembled before him.

"But forms are nothing when substance has gone, and the forms of popular government are those from which the substance of freedom may most easily go. Extremes meet, and a government of universal suffrage and theoretical equality may, under conditions which impel the change, most readily become a despotism. For there, despotism advances in the name and with the might of the people. . . And when the disparity of condition increases, so does universal suffrage make it easy to seize the source of power, for the greater is the proportion of power in the hands of those who feel no direct interest in the conduct of government; who, tortured by want and embruted by poverty, are ready to sell their votes to the highest bidder or follow the lead of the most blatant demagogue; or who, made bitter by hardships, may even look upon profligate and tyrannous government with the satisfaction we may imagine the proletarians and slaves of Rome to have felt, as they saw a Caligula or Nero raging among the rich patricians. . . Now, this transformation of popular government into despotism of the vilest and most degrading kind, which must inevitably result from the unequal distribution of wealth, is not a thing of the far future. It has already begun in the United States, and is rapidly going on under our eyes. . . The type of modern growth is the great city. Here are to be found the greatest wealth and the deepest poverty. And it is here that popular government has most clearly broken down. . . In theory we are intense democrats. . . But is there not growing up among us a class who have all the power without any of the virtues of aristocracy? . . . Industry everywhere tends to assume a form in which one is master and many serve. And when one is master and the others serve, the one will control the others, even in such matters as votes. . . There is no mistaking it—the very foundations of society are being sapped before our eyes. . . It is shown in greatest force where the inequalities in the distribution of wealth are greatest, and it shows itself as they increase. . . Though we may not speak of it openly, the general faith in republican institutions is, where they have reached their fullest development, narrowing and weakening. It is no longer that confident belief in republicanism as the source of national blessings that it once was. Thoughtful men are beginning to see its dangers, without seeing how to escape them; are beginning to accept the view of Macaulay and distrust that of Jefferson. And the people at large are becoming used to the growing corruption. The most ominous political sign in the United States to-day is the growth of a sentiment which either doubts the existence of an honest man in public office or looks on him as a fool for not seizing his opportunities. . . Thus in the United States to-day is republican government running the course it must inevitably follow under conditions which cause the unequal distribution of wealth."—*Progress and Poverty*, book x, ch. iv.

study and other tutoring, but *thought*."⁴¹ To jump at a conclusion is very likely to jump over the cause, at which no class is more apt than the tutored class."⁴² We must proceed step by step from familiar and indisputable premises.

1. THE SOURCE OF WEALTH.

The first demand upon us is to make sure that we know the source of the things that satisfy want."⁴³ But it is quite unnecessary to tediously specify these and

---

41. "The power to reason correctly on general subjects is not to be learned in schools, nor does it come with special knowledge. It results from care in separating, from caution in combining, from the habit of asking ourselves the meaning of the words we use, and making sure of one step before building another upon it—and above all, from loyalty to truth."—*Henry George's Perplexed Philosopher, p. 9.*

42. "Harold Frederic, the London correspondent of the New York *Times*, reports Mr. Gladstone as having said in substance, in one of his campaign speeches, that the older he grew the more he began to conclude that the highly educated classes were in public affairs rather more conspicuously foolish than anybody else. Mr. Frederic thinks that the Tories have since done much to ' breed a suspicion that therein Gladstone touched the outskirts of a great and solemn truth.' But it needed not the action of the Tories to breed that suspicion. In this country as well as in England it is patent to any close observer that the highly educated classes, or to speak with more exactness, the highly *tutored* classes, when compared with the common people, are in public affairs but little better than fools. The explanation is simple. The common people are philosophers unencumbered with useless knowledge, who look upon public affairs broadly, and moralists who pry beneath the surface of custom and precedent into the heart of public questions. The minds of the tutored classes, on the contrary, are dwarfed by close attention to particulars to the exclusion of generals, and distorted by such false morality as is involved in tutorial notions regardi g vested rights."—*The Standard*, July 27, 1892.

The tendency of tutoring to elevate mere authority above observation and thought is well illustrated by the story of two classes in a famous school. The primary class, being asked if fishes have eyelids, went to the aquarium and observed ; the senior class being asked the same question, went to the library and consulted authorities.

"One may stand on a box and look over the heads of his fellows, but he no better sees the stars. The telescope and the microscope reveal depths which to the unassisted vision are closed. Yet not merely do they bring us no nearer to the cause of suns and animalcula, but in looking through them the observer must shut his eyes to what lies about him. . . . A man of special learning may be a fool as to common relations."—*Perplexed Philosopher, Introduction.*

43. For it is ability or inability to satisfy his wants that determines whether or not a man is poor. He who has the power to procure what he wants, as he wants it, and in satisfactory quality and quantity, is not poor. No matter how he gets the power, provided he keeps out of the penitentiary, he is accounted rich.

trace them to their origin in detail. In searching for the source of one we shall discover the source of all.

As a common object of this kind, the production of which is a familiar process, bread is probably the best example for our purpose. Let us, then, carefully trace bread to its source. To make the results of our work clear to the eye as well as to the ear we will construct a chart as we proceed. The chart should begin with a classification of Bread with reference to Man, for it is as an object for satisfying the wants of man that we consider bread at all. Is Bread a part of the personality of Man? or is it an object external to him? That is our first question. The answer is so obvious that a child could make no mistake. Bread is external to Man. It should, therefore, be classified with what for brevity we will call "External Objects." It is also a *product* having certain *constituents*.

Let us so arrange the chart as to indicate these facts and also to provide a place for particularizing the constituents of bread as we ascertain them. Thus:

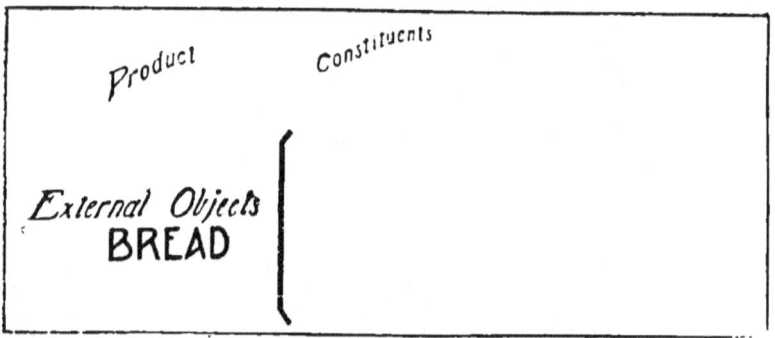

Now let the necessary constituents of bread be inserted. Any housewife, any kitchen girl, knows what they are as well as does the most expert baker or learned chemist. They are named in the place reserved for them in the chart:

Product	Constituents	
External Objects **BREAD**	{ A BAKER A LOT o' LAND AN OVEN A FIRE FLOUR YEAST SALT WATER }	FOR THE OVEN AND THE BAKER TO STAND ON

In respect of Man the constituents of Bread all fall into two general classes: Man, and objects that are external to him—or, briefly, External Objects. Thus:

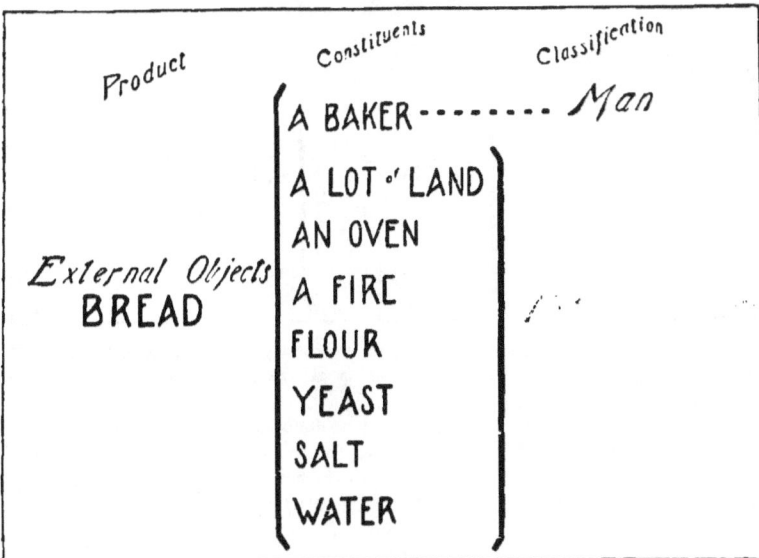

While all these External Objects are alike in the one particular that they are external to Man, some of them may differ from others in respects which, for clear thinking, must be distinguished. Compare the first two External Objects—the lot of land and the oven—and a radical difference at once appears. The lot of land is a *natural* object. The oven is an *artificial* object. The lot exists independently of man's art; the oven can have no existence whatever as an oven but for man's art." And when the remaining External Objects are considered the same difference appears. All of them, Bread included, differ from the lot of land precisely as the oven does; they are artificial. Let us note this difference upon our chart:

Product	Constituents	Classification
Artificial External Objects **BREAD**	A BAKER	*Man*
	A LOT of LAND	
	AN OVEN	
	A FIRE	
	FLOUR	*Artificial External Objects*
	YEAST	
	SALT	
	WATER	

44. This difference is frequently ignored, even by political economists; but it is plain to any intelligent mind that no reasoning can be trusted which does not distinguish a difference so radical.

45. As to the flour and the yeast, there is no doubt of this. And though not so obvious, it is equally true of the fire, which but for the art of man would not exist in the oven; of the water, which but for that would not be at hand; and of the salt, which without man's art would be neither in proper form nor place. It follows that,

It is no longer necessary to name the specific constituents of Bread, and we may simplify the chart by erasing them, together with the word "bread" itself, retaining only the class names. It will be more appropriate, too, if we substitute the term "factors" for the term "classification." Thus:

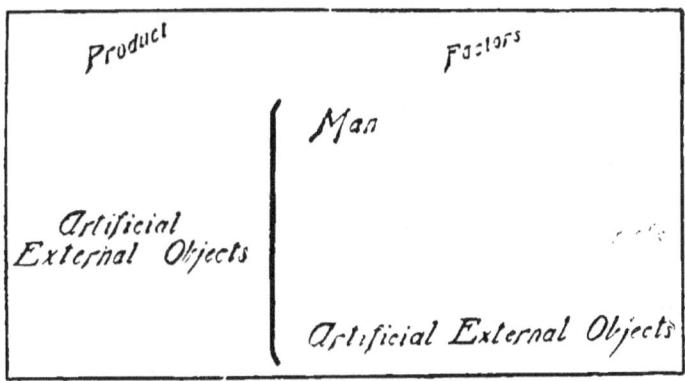

Grave danger of confusion here arises. Artificial Objects, it will be seen, are classified both as the "product" and as a "factor." Yet it cannot be that any factor of a product is exactly the same as the product; there is surely some difference which we should try to discover.

Turn to the chart on page 30, which specifies the artificial constituents of Bread, namely: oven, fire, flour, yeast, salt, water. How do these artificial factors differ from the artificial product, bread? Simply in this, that the artificial factors are *unfinished* bread, while the product is *finished* bread.[46] The difference,

either as to form or place or both, all the external objects, except the lot of land, are artificial. The bread itself is of course artificial.

46. It is because man desires bread that he constructs ovens, builds fires in them, grinds flour, digs or evaporates salt, prepares yeast, or carries water to the dough-trough. And going farther back, it is because he desires bread that he raises grain, erects mills, and produces machinery for bread-making. This is plain enough in a

then, between artificial objects as a factor, and artificial objects as a final product, is that the former are unfinished and the latter are finished. Let us note the distinction:

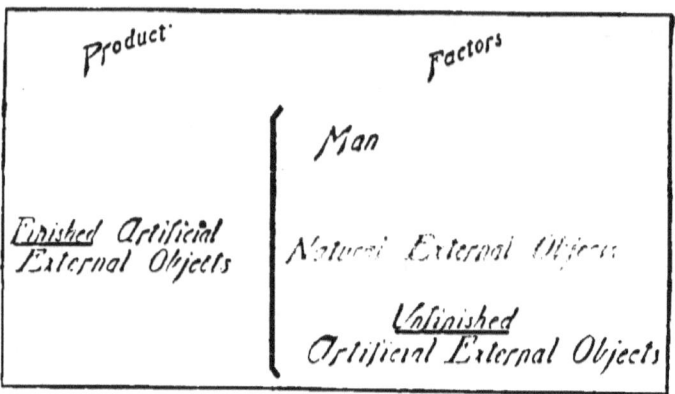

The language of the chart may now be supplemented with the technical terms that political economists adopt, which, when comprehended and used with discrimination, distinguish the differences we

community of one like that of Robinson Crusoe. But it is just as true in a community of millions. In the community of one the solitary individual performs all the steps necessary to produce bread because *he* wants bread. In the great society individuals divide their work, some doing one part and others other parts; but the motive, still the same, is the desire of the community for bread. All the processes of industry to the extent that they are directed to the production of bread, whether they be in the departments of mining, of lumbering, of railroading, of navigation, of engineering, of farming, of storekeeping, of baking, or what not, are steps or stages in bread-making; and every artificial object produced for the purpose of facilitating bread-making is to that extent unfinished bread. But bread itself, from the time it comes into the possession of the consumer (for it is not complete until the final deliverer has accomplished his work regarding it), is a finished object. The essential difference, then, between the artificial objects that are classified as "product" and those that are classified as "factors" is that the former are finished and the latter are unfinished.

Professor Marshall (*Marshall's Prin., book ii, ch. iii.*) divides artificial objects into "goods of the first order, which satisfy wants directly, such as food, clothing, etc.; goods of the second order, such as flour mills, which satisfy wants, not directly but indirectly, by contributing toward the production of goods of the first order"; and "goods of the third order," under which he arranges "all things that are used for making goods of the second order, such as the machinery for making milling machinery." He says we might carry the analysis further if necessary. And so we

have discovered with equal precision and greater brevity than the more cumbrous terms upon which we have so far relied."⁷ Thus:

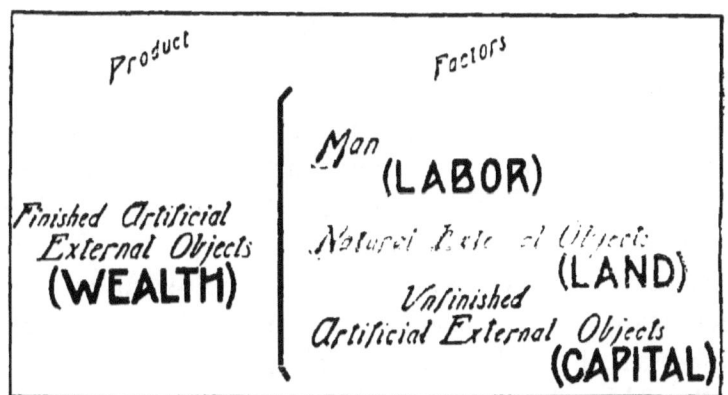

At this point we find all essential differences distinguished. Every factor of industry and every material object of desire that can be imagined falls into one or

might. We might drag it out into an interminable catalogue; but every item would be an unfinished artificial object, and for all purposes of economic reasoning nothing else. His own classification into "consumers' goods" (finished artificial objects), and "producers' goods" (unfinished artificial objects) is complete.

47. It makes no difference what terms are adopted, for they serve only as symbols; but it is of vital importance that the same terms shall never symbolize things that essentially differ. As the technical terms that usage forces upon us in connection with our subject are also loose colloquial words, they are especially liable to abuse in this respect. The term "wealth" is a bewildering example. It has been used to symbolize as of one class such diverse things as building lots, houses, farm sites, farm improvements, deeds, mortgages, promissory notes, warehouse receipts and the goods they call for, book accounts, and slaves, thus confusing three or four different kinds of things, instead of distinguishing one kind from all others. Made to include building lots and farm sites, the term is a symbol for natural objects; made to include houses, farm improvements, and goods, it is a symbol for artificial objects; by including slaves it symbolizes man; and by including deeds, promissory notes, warehouse receipts, and book accounts, it symbolizes nothing but evidences of legal title as between individual men. When the same term is used to include things so essentially different as natural objects external to man, artificial objects external to man, man himself, and *indicia* of title, it is hopeless to attempt to reason about the mutual relations of those things.

another of the four classes of the chart." And from mere inspection of the chart we may see, what was promised when we began its construction, that in searching for the source of one of the objects that satisfy human wants we have discovered the source of all. For it is self-evident that the material wants of men are satisfied in no other way than by the consumption of finished artificial objects, technically termed Wealth; and the chart shows that such objects have their source in a combination of the three "factors," namely: (1) the activities of man, technically termed Labor; (2) natural objects external to man, technically termed Land; and (3) unfinished artificial objects, technically termed Capital.

But while these three factors combined produce all the material objects that tend to satisfy human wants, they do not constitute the *ultimate* source of those objects. Our analysis is not yet ended; our chart is still incomplete.

Reflection assures us that all artificial objects, finished and unfinished, resolve upon final analysis into the two factors, the activities of man and natural external objects; or, in technical language, all Wealth,

---

48. For example: Flour, which is unfinished bread, and therefore unfinished wealth—Capital, appears upon analysis to be a compound of grain, a mill site, and a miller. The mill site and the miller are respectively land and labor; but the grain and the mill are unfinished wealth—Capital, and map be further analyzed. Passing the mill for the moment to analyze the grain, we find it composed of a farmer, a farm site, and farming improvements and implements. The farm site, like the mill site, is land; and the farmer, like the miller, is labor; but the improvements and implements, like the mill and the grain, are unfinished wealth—Capital, and may be still further analyzed. And so on.

If analyzed to the last, every constituent of bread, and every constituent of that constituent, would resolve into labor and land. To follow them step by step would be tedious work and require much special knowledge. It would involve consideration of factories and factory sites, stores and store sites, railroads and railroad sites, mining and mines, lumbering and forests, rivers, docks, oceans, and ships. But analysis in full detail is not necessary. The conclusion is self-evident the moment it is understood.

finished and unfinished, resolves upon final analysis into Labor and Land. Therefore, Capital is in final analysis eliminated as a factor of production. It expresses nothing which the two remaining factors do not imply; for it is by the conjunction of those two factors that Capital itself is produced.[19] Unfinished artificial objects and their technical term, Capital, should, therefore, be erased from the chart. Following is the result:

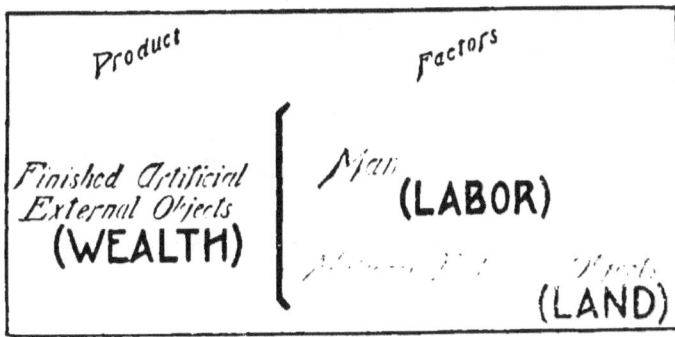

Thus all artificial objects external to man—Wealth, are found to have their ultimate source in the conjunction of man's activities—Labor, with natural objects external to man—Land.

[49.] The primary error in all forms of socialism consists in ignoring the fact that Capital is but a product of labor and land; or what in effect is the same thing, in disregarding the necessary inference that land is the only implement of labor. Intelligent socialists insist that they do not ignore it; but that, while acknowledging land to be the primary implement of labor, they see in this only an abstract formula, having at the present stage of civilization no practical importance. Society, they urge, is impossible without Capital; and he who would live in society must have Capital, or be the slave of those who do have it. Therefore, they argue, Capital is in the social state as indispensable as land. Their reasoning hinges upon the mistaken assumption that Capital is an accumulation of the past instead of being a product of the present. As one socialistic author puts it, "Though labor may originally have preceded Capital, yet it is now as absurd to place one before the other as it is to attempt to say whether the hen originates the egg or the egg the hen." The explanation of division of labor and trade, the effect of which is overlooked by socialistic philosophies, affords a better opportunity than the present for considering this elementary error of socialism, and a brief discussion of the subject will be given in that connection. See *post*, note 81.

Finally, by dropping the cumbrous language altogether, and using only the technical terms, we complete our chart.[50] Thus:

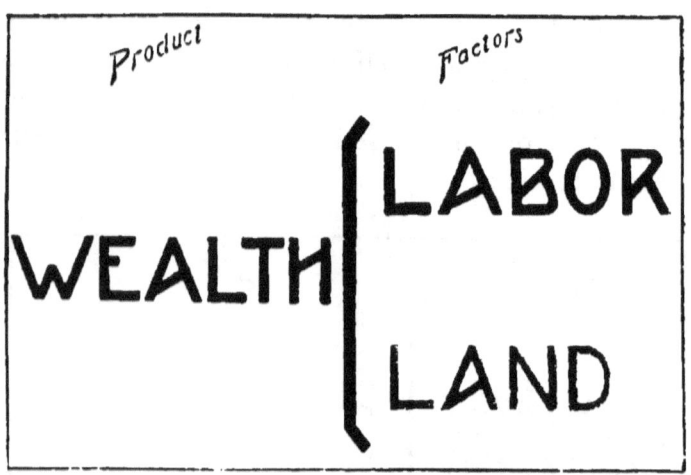

The chart may be read as follows:

Wealth is produced solely by the application of Labor to Land.[51]

> 50. It may at first seem like a great waste of time and space to have gone through this long analysis for no other purpose at last than to demonstrate the self-evident fact that land and labor are the sole original factors in the production of Wealth. But it will have been no waste if it enables the reader to firmly grasp the fact. Nothing is more obvious, to be sure. Nothing is more readily assented to. Yet by layman and college professor and economic author alike, this simple truth is cast adrift at the very threshold of argument or investigation, with results akin to what might be expected in physics if after recognizing the law of gravitation its effects should be completely ignored.
>
> 51. There is ample authority among economic writers for this conclusion.
>
> Professor Ely enumerates Nature, Labor, and Capital as the factors of production, but he describes Capital as a combination of Nature and Labor.—*Ely's Introduction, part ii, ch. iii.*
>
> Say describes industry as "nothing more or less than human employment of natural agents."—*Say's Trea., book i, ch. ii.*
>
> And though John Stuart Mill and numerous others speak of Land, Labor, and Capital as the three factors of production, as does Professor Jevons, most of them, like Jevons, recognize the fact, though in their reasoning they often fail to profit by it, that Capital is not a primary but a secondary requisite. See *Jevons's Pol. Ec., secs.* 16, 19.
>
> Henry George says : " Land, labor, and capital are the factors of production. The

This is the final analysis. In the union of Labor, which includes all human effort,[52] with Land, which includes the whole material universe outside of man,[53] we discover the ultimate source of Wealth, which includes all the material things that satisfy want.[54] And that is the first great truth upon which the single tax philosophy is built.

2. THE PRODUCTION OF WEALTH.

When considered in connection with primitive modes of production, the vital importance of this truth is self-evident.[55] If those modes prevailed, involuntary

term land includes all natural opportunities or forces; the term labor, all human exertion; andthe term capital, all wealth used to produce more wealth. . . Capital is not a necessary factor in production. Labor exerted upon land can produce wealth without the aid of capital, and in the necessary genesis of things must so produce wealth before capital can exist."—*Progress and Poverty, book iii, ch. i.*

Also: "The complexities of production in the civilized state, in which so great a part is borne by exchange, and so much labor is bestowed upon materials after they have been separated from the land, though they may to the unthinking disguise, do not alter the fact that all production is still the union of the two factors, land and labor."—*Id., ch. viii.*

By intelligent observers no authority is needed. In all the phenomena of human life, whether primitive or civilized, the lesson of the chart stands out in bold relief. Nothing can be produced without Labor and Land, and nothing can be named which under any circumstances enters into productive processes that is not resolvable into either the one or the other. To satisfy all human wants mankind requires nothing but human labor and natural material, and each of them is indispensable.

52. "The term labor includes all human exertion in the production of wealth."—*Progress and Poverty, book i, ch. ii.*

53. "The term land necessarily includes, not merely the surface of the earth as distinguished from the water and the air, but the whole material universe outside of man himself, for it is only by having access to land, from which his very body is drawn, that man can come in contact with or use nature."—*Progress and Poverty, book i, ch. ii.*

54. "As commonly used the word 'wealth' is applied to anything having exchange value. But . . . wealth, as alone the term can be used in political economy, consists of natural products that have been secured, moved, combined, separated, or in other ways modified by human exertion, so as to fit them for the gratification of human desires."—*Progress and Poverty, book i, ch. ii.*

55. If we imagine upon a lonely island a solitary man, without capital, without clothing, without adequate shelter, what would be our explanation of his poverty? We certainly should not say that it was caused by a superabundance of goods—by over-production; nor should we be any more likely to attribute it to scarcity of money. We should first ask if the land of the island were barren. Upon being

poverty would be readily traced either to direct enslavement through ownership of Labor, or to indirect enslavement through ownership of Land." There could be no other cause. If both causes were absent, every indi-

assured that it would yield far more than the solitary inhabitant could consume, we should ask if he were physically or mentally incapable of producing the things he required. If told that not only was he quite capable, but that in the years he had been upon the island he had continually improved in industrial knowledge, in inventive acuteness, in manual dexterity, and in muscular power, and yet that he was scarcely if any better able to satisfy his wants than when first cast ashore, we might ask if he were lazy. If informed that he was not lazy, that he worked almost as many hours as ever and quite as hard and far more productively, we should ask if he were the chattel slave of an exacting master. Satisfied that this was not the case, we should then say :

"The only explanation left is that in some way that man's opportunities to use the island are restricted—the Labor of the island and the Land of the island do not freely meet."

And if we were thereupon advised that a neighboring cannibal chief, who claimed the island as his private property, had granted the lone inhabitant permission to live, upon the sole condition that he yield tribute for the land, and that the tribute had a way of advancing as the worker's productive power increased, we should understand the cause of his poverty. And we should advise him to find a way at once of throwing off the land-owner's yoke, and to postpone all such secondary questions as the money supply until their proper settlement could operate for his own benefit instead of for the benefit of the proprietor of the island.

56. The ownership of the land is essentially the ownership of the men who must use it.

"Let the circumstances be what they may—the ownership of land will always give the ownership of men to a degree measured by the necessity (real or artificial) for the use of land. . . Place one hundred men on an island from which there is no escape, and whether you make one of these men the absolute owner of the other ninety-nine, or the absolute owner of the soil of the island, will make no difference either to him or to them."—*Progress and Poverty, book vii, ch. ii.*

Let us imagine a shipwrecked sailor who, after battling with the waves, touches land upon an uninhabited but fertile island. Though hungry and naked and shelterless, he soon has food and clothing and a house—all of them rude, to be sure, but comfortable. How does he get them ? By applying his Labor to the Land of the island. In a little while he lives as comfortably as an isolated man can.

Now let another shipwrecked sailor be washed ashore. As he is about to step out of the water the first man accosts him :

"Hello, there ! If you want to come ashore you must agree to be my slave."

The second replies :

"I can't. I come from the United States, where they don't believe in slavery."

"Oh, I beg your pardon. I didn't know you came from the United States. I had no intention of hurting your feelings, you know. But say, they believe in owning land in the United States, don't they ? "

"Yes."

"Very well ; you just agree that this island is mine, and you may come ashore a free man."

vidual might, if he wished, enjoy all the Wealth that his own powers were capable of producing in the primitive modes of production and under the limitations of common knowledge that belonged to his environment.[57]

"But how does the island happen to be yours? Did you make it?"
"No, I didn't make it."
"Have you a title from its maker?"
"No, I haven't any title from its maker."
"Well, what is your title, anyhow?"
"Oh, my title is good enough. I got here first."
Of course he got there first. But he didn't mean to, and he wouldn't have done it if he could have helped it. But the newcomer is satisfied, and says:
"Well, that's a good United States title, so I guess I'll recognize it and come ashore. But remember, I am to be a free man."
"Certainly you are. Come right along up to my cabin."
For a time the two get along well enough together. But on some fine morning the proprietor concludes that he would rather lie abed than scurry around for his breakfast; and not being in a good humor, perhaps, he somewhat roughly commands his "brother man" to cook him a bird.
"What?" exclaims the brother.
"I tell you to go and kill a bird and cook it for my breakfast."
"That sounds big," sneers the second free and equal member of the little community; "but what am I to get for doing this?"
"Oh," the first replies languidly, "if you kill me a fat bird and cook it nicely, then after I have had my breakfast off the bird you may cook the gizzard for your own breakfast. That's pay enough. The work is easy."
"But I want you to understand that I am not your slave, and I won't do that work for that pay. I'll do as much work for you as you do for me, and no more."
"Then, sir," the first comer shouts in virtuous wrath, "I want you to understand that my charity is at an end. I have treated you better than you deserved in the past, and this is your gratitude. Now I don't propose to have any loafers on my property. You will work for the wages I offer or get off my land! You are perfectly free. Take the wages or leave them. Do the work or let it alone. There is no slavery here. But if you are not satisfied with my terms, leave my island!"
The second man, if accustomed to the usages of the labor unions, would probably go out and, to the music of his own violent language about the "greed of capital," destroy as many bows and arrows as he could, so as to paralyze the bird-shooting industry; and this proceeding he would call a strike for honest wages and the dignity of labor. If he were accustomed to social reform notions of the namby-pamby variety, he would propose an arbitration, and be mildly indignant when told that there was nothing to arbitrate—that he had only to accept the other's offer or get off his property. But if a sensible man, he would notify his comrade that the privilege of owning islands in that latitude had expired.

57. While in the Pennsylvania coal regions a few years ago I was told of an incident that illustrates the power of perpetuating poverty which resides in the absolute ownership of land.

The miners were in poverty. Despite the lavish protection bestowed upon them by tariff laws at the solicitation of monopolies which dictate our tariff policy, the men were afflicted with poverty in many forms. They were poor as to clothing, poor as to

But in the civilized state this principle is so entangled in the complexities of division of labor and trade as to be almost lost in the maze. Many, even of those who recognize it, fail to grasp it as a fundamental truth. Yet it is no less vital in civilized than in primitive modes of production.

a. *Division of Labor.*

The essential difference between primitive and civilized modes of production is not in the accumulation of capital which characterizes the latter, but in the greater scope and minuteness of its division of labor.[58] Capital is an effect of division of labor rather than a cause. Division of labor, by enhancing labor power and relieving man from the perpetual pursuit of mere subsistence, utilizes capital and makes civilization possible.[59]

shelter, poor as to food, and to be more specific, they were in extreme poverty as to ice. When the summer months came they lacked this thing because they could not afford to buy, and they suffered.

Owing to the undermining of the ground and the caving in of the surface here and there, there were great holes into which the snow and the rain fell in winter and froze, forming a passable quality of ice. Now it is frequently said that intelligence, industry, and thrift will abolish poverty. But these virtues were not successful among the men of whom I speak. They were intelligent enough to see that this ice if they saved it would abolish their poverty as to ice, and they were industrious enough and thrifty enough not only to be willing to save it, but actually to begin the work. Preparing little caves to preserve the ice in, they went into the holes after a long day's work in the mines, and gathered what so far as the need of ice was concerned was to abolish their poverty in the ensuing summer. But the owner of this part of the earth—a man who had neither made the earth, nor the rain, nor the snow, nor the ice, nor even the hole—telegraphed his agent forbidding the removal of ice except upon payment of a certain sum per ton.

The miners couldn't afford the condition. They controlled the necessary Labor, and were willing to give it to abolish their poverty; but the Land was placed beyond their reach by an owner, and in consequence of that, and not from any lack of intelligence, industry, or thrift on their own part, their poverty as to ice was perpetuated.

58. It is his failure to realize this that accounts for the theory of the socialist that laborers in the civilized state are dependent upon accumulated capital as well as upon land for opportunities to produce. See *ante*, note 49, and *post*, note 81.

59. Here are two men at a given point. Each has an errand to do a mile to the east, and each has one to do a mile to the west. If each goes upon his own errand each will travel a mile out and a mile back in one direction and the same in the other, making four miles' travel apiece, or eight miles in all. But if one does both errands to

The productive power of division of labor may be illustrated by considering it as a means for utilizing differences of soil and climate. If, for example, the soil and the climate of two sections of a country, or of two different countries (for the effects of division of labor are not dependent upon political geography[59]), differ inversely, one being better adapted to the production of corn than of sugar, and the other, on the contrary, being better adapted to the production of sugar than of corn, they will yield more wealth in corn and sugar with division of labor than without it.

Let us imagine a Mainland and an Island, which, as to the adaptability of their soil and climate to the production of corn and sugar, so differ that if the people of each should raise their own corn and their own sugar they would produce, with a given unit of labor force, but 22 of Wealth—11 in corn and 11 in sugar. Thus:

	CORN	SUGAR	TOTAL
MAINLAND	10	1	11
ISLAND	1	10	11
TOTAL	11	11	22

the east and the other does both to the west, they will travel but two miles apiece, or four in all. By division of labor they free half their energy and half their time for devotion to other work, or to study, or to play, as their inclinations dictate.

60. No more than are the effects of a healthful climate. Protectionists who argue that there should be free trade between villages, cities, counties and states in the same nation, but protection for nations, thus making the effect of trade to depend upon the invisible political boundary line that separates communities, are like the colored woman who, when her house, without being physically removed, had been politically shifted from North Carolina to Virginia by a change of the boundary line, expressed

Production in that manner would ignore the opportunities afforded by nature to man for utilizing differences of soil and climate; but by such a wise division as Labor would adopt in similar circumstances, if unrestrained, the same unit of labor force almost doubles the product. Thus:

	CORN	SUGAR	TOTAL
MAINLAND	20		20
ISLAND	0	20	20
TOTAL	20		40

Nor is it alone because it utilizes differences of soil and climate that division of labor is so effective. Its effectiveness is enhanced in still higher degree by its lessening of the labor force necessary to accomplish any industrial result, whether in mining, manufacturing, transporting, store-keeping, professional employments, agriculture, or the incidental occupations. Minute division of labor, instead of accounting for poverty in the civilized state, makes it all the more unaccountable.

b. Trade.

But division of labor is dependent upon trade. If trade were wholly stopped there would be no division of labor;" if it be interfered with, division of labor is

---

her satisfaction in the remark that she was very glad of it, because she "allus yearn tail dot dat yah Nof Kline was an a'mighty sickly State," and she was glad that she didn't "live dyeah no mo'!"

61. Men who devoted themselves to specialties, unable to exchange their products for the objects of their desire, which alone would be the motive for their special labor, would abandon specialties and resort to less civilized methods of supplying their wants.

obstructed.[62] In the last preceding chart, which illustrates the effect of division of labor without trade, the Mainland gets 20 of corn, but no sugar, and the Island gets 20 of sugar, but no corn. Yet each wants both sugar and corn; and if they freely trade, their wants in these respects will be better satisfied than if each raises its own corn and sugar.

Compare the first chart of this series with the following:[63]

	CORN	SUGAR	TOTAL
MAINLAND	19		20
ISLAND	1		20
TOTAL	20	2	40

The comparison[64] illustrates the advantage to each individual, community and country, of division of labor and trade over more primitive modes of production.

62. Division of labor, whether adopted to take advantage of the different varieties of land, or to secure the benefits of special skill in labor, cannot continue without trade; and to the degree that trade is impeded, to that degree division of labor will languish. It is only under absolute free trade between all people and in respect of all products that division of labor can flourish. Any interference with it is economically an enslavement of labor in a degree proportioned to the degree of interference.

63. It will be seen from this chart that the people of the two places, by dividing their given expenditure of labor in such a manner as to utilize the natural advantage peculiar to each place, secure a clear profit of 18. And this is a substantial profit, consisting not merely of figures upon paper, but of real wealth—artificial external objects which serve to satisfy human desires.

64. The people of the Mainland have now sent 10 of their corn to the Island, and the people of the Island have paid for it by sending 10 of their sugar to the Mainland. For simplicity, the cost of effecting the trade is omitted. It does not affect the principle. If the cost were so high that more sugar and corn could be got without division of labor than with, division of labor would be abandoned as unprofitable; if low enough to admit of any profit at all, the trading would go on, unless restrained, precisely as if it involved no cost. It may be well to state, however, that the nearer we get to no cost in trading, the better are we off. Hence, any tariff on trading,

It is like the difference between raising weights by direct application of power, and by means of block and tackle.[65]

And what this series of charts illustrates regarding two places and two forms of wealth, is true in principle of all places and all forms of wealth. That every one is better served when each does for others what relatively he does best, in exchange for what relatively they do best, is as true of communities and nations as it is of individuals. Indeed, it is true of communities and nations *because* it is true of individuals; for it is individuals that trade, and not communities or nations as such.[66]

whether domestic or foreign, like railroad and shipping rates for freight, is prejudicial; for tariffs add to the cost of trading just as freight rates do. Protection has that for its object. When it does not add enough to the price of a foreign product to prevent importation it fails of its purpose. And though revenue tariffs have no such object they produce the same effect, only in minor degree.

65. If every man were obliged, unassisted by the co-operation of others, to supply his own needs directly by his own labor, few could more than meagerly satisfy even the simplest of those desires which we have in common with lower animals. Though each labored diligently the aggregate of wealth would be exceedingly small compared with the necessities of those who wished to consume it, while in variety it would be very limited and in quality of the poorest kind. But by division of labor, which has been carried to marvelous lengths and is still developing, productive power is so enormously increased that the annual wealth products of the present time, in quantity and quality, in variety, usefulness and beauty, almost appear to be the work of giants and fairies.

66. Mankind as a whole may be likened to a great man, with eyes to see, brain to invent and direct, nerves for intercommunication, and various muscles for various actions. As different parts of the bodies of men do different things, each part contributing co-operatively to a general result, so it is with the body politic, whose different parts—individual men—contribute in different ways to the common good. Trade is to the body politic what digestion is to the physical body. To prohibit it is to deprive the great man of his stomach; to restrict it is to give him dyspepsia.

Says Emerson in the "American Scholar," an oration delivered at Cambridge in 1837: "It is one of those fables which out of an unknown antiquity convey an unlooked-for wisdom, that the gods, in the beginning, divided man into men, that he might be more helpful to himself; just as the hand was divided into fingers, the better to answer its ends."

Reflection upon the labor-saving power of trade makes it clear that the notion of protectionists that free trade is prejudicial to home industry has no foundation. It would interfere with "home industries" that could be better conducted elsewhere; but by that very fact it would strengthen the industries that belonged at home.

c. The Law of Division of Labor and Trade.

Now, what is it that leads men to conform their conduct to the principle illustrated by the last chart? Why do they divide their labor, and trade its products? A simple, universal and familiar law of human nature moves them. Whether men be isolated, or be living in primitive communities, or in advanced states of civilization, their *demand for consumption determines the direction of Labor in production.*[67] That is the law.

When we decide to buy foreign goods we do not thereby decide to employ foreign labor instead of American labor; we decide that the American labor shall be employed in making things to trade for what we buy, instead of making the things that we buy. And we get a better net result or we wouldn't do it.

Free trade and labor-saving machinery, which belong in the same industrial category, increase the aggregate wealth of the country where they flourish. Whether or not they tend to impoverish individuals or classes, depends upon the manner in which the increased wealth is distributed. If they do so tend, the remedy surely does not lie in the direction of obstructing trade and smashing machines so that less wealth may be produced with given labor, but in altering the conditions that promote unjust distribution.

67. The term "production" means not creation but adaptation. Man cannot add an atom to the universe of matter; but he can so modify the condition of matter, both in respect of form and of place, as to adapt it to the satisfaction of human desires. To do this is to produce wealth.

"Consumption" is the ultimate object of all production. We produce because we desire to consume. But consumption does not mean destruction. Man has no more power to destroy than to create. His power in consumption, like his power in production, is limited to changing the condition of things. As by production man changes things from natural to artificial conditions to satisfy his desires, so by consumption he changes things from artificial to natural conditions in the process of satisfying his desires.

Production is the drawing forth of desired things, of Wealth, from the Land; consumption is the returning back of those things to the Land.

"All labor is but the movement of particles of matter from one place to another."—*Dick's Outlines, p.* 25.

Production consists merely in changing things.—*Ely's Intro., part ii, ch. i; Mill's Prin., book i, ch. i, sec.* 2.

"As man creates no new matter but only utilities, so he destroys no matter, but only utilities. Consumption means the destruction of a utility."—*Ely's Intro., part v, ch. i, p.* 268.

Production means "drawing forth."—*Jevons's Primer, sec.* 17.

"Man cannot create material things... His efforts and sacrifices result in changing the form or arrangement of matter to adapt it better for the satisfaction of wants."—*Marshall's Prin., book ii, ch. iii, sec.* 1.

"It is sometimes said that traders do not produce; that while the cabinet maker

Considered in connection with a solitary individual, like Robinson Crusoe upon his island, it is obvious. What he demanded for consumption he was obliged to produce. Even as to the goods he collected from stranded ships—desiring to consume them, he was obliged to labor to produce them to places of safety. His demand for consumption always determined the direction of his labor in production.[68] And when we remember that what Robinson Crusoe was to his island in the sea, civilized man as a whole is to this island in space, we may readily understand the application of the same simple law to the great body of labor in the civilized world.[69] Nevertheless, the com-

produces furniture, the furniture dealer merely sells what is already produced. But there is no scientific foundation for this distinction."—*Id.*

" As his [man's] production of material products is really nothing more than a rearrangement of matter which gives it new utilities, so his consumption of them is nothing more than a disarrangement of matter which diminishes or destroys its utilities."—*Id.*

" In like manner as by production is meant the creation not of substance but of utility, so by consumption is meant the destruction of utility and not of substance or matter."—*Say's Trea., book ii, ch. i.*

" All that man can do is to reproduce existing materials under another form, which may give them a utility they did not before possess, or merely enlarge one they may have before presented. So that in fact there is a creation not of matter but of utility ; and this I call production of wealth. . . There is no actual production of wealth without a creation or augmentation of utility."—*Say's Trea., book i, ch. i.*

68. It is highly significant that while Robinson Crusoe had unsatisfied wants he was never out of a job.

69. Demand for consumption is satisfied not from hoards of accumulated wealth, but from the stream of current production. Broadly speaking there can be no accumulation of wealth in the sense of saving up wealth from generation to generation. Imagine a man's satisfying his demand for eggs from the accumulated stores of his ancestors! Yet eggs do not differ in this respect from other forms of wealth, except that some other forms will keep a little longer, and some not so long.

The notion that a saving instinct must be aroused before the great and more lasting forms of wealth can be brought forth is a mistake. Houses and locomotives, for example, are built not because of any desire to accumulate wealth, but because we need houses to live in and locomotives to transport us and our goods. It is not the *saving*, but the *serving*, instinct that induces the production of these things; the same instinct that induces the production of a loaf of bread.

Artificial things do not save. No sooner are the processes of production from land complete than the products are on their way back to the land. If man does not return them by means of consumption, then through decay they return themselves. Man-

plexities of civilized life are so likely to obscure its operation and disguise its relations to social questions like that of the persistence of poverty as to make illustration desirable.

The following chart classifies about every kind of wealth that man requires, and also "personal services," which, though as useful as wealth, do not crystallize in material products—such services as those of lawyers, barbers, doctors, teachers, actors, and so on:

The circle of variegated colors represents the com-

kind as a whole lives literally from hand to mouth. What is demanded for consumption in the present must be produced by the labor of the present. From current production, and from that alone, can current consumption be satisfied.

"Accumulated wealth" is, in fact, not wealth at all in any great degree. It is merely titles to wealth yet to be produced. A share in a mining company, for example, is but a certificate that the owner is legally entitled to a proportion of the wealth to be produced in the future from a certain mine.

Titles to future wealth may be both morally and legally valid. This is so when they represent past labor or its products loaned in free contract for future labor or its products; for example, a contract for the delivery of goods of any kind to-day to be paid for next week, or next month, or next year, or in ten years, or later.

They may be legally but not morally valid. This is so when they represent the product of a franchise (whether paid for in labor or not) to exact tribute from future labor; for example, a franchise to confiscate a man's labor through ownership of his body, as in slavery, or a franchise to confiscate the products of labor in general through ownership of land.

Or they may be both legally and morally invalid, as when they are obtained by illegal force or fraud from the rightful owner.

mercial reservoir into which Wealth is poured by production, and from which it is drawn for consumption, each color typifying the kind of wealth or service named in it. Now, let us suppose that Personal Servants tap the commercial reservoir for food. They do it by applying at retail stores for what will relieve their poverty as to food, and food flows out to them[70] as indicated by the blue arrow, which we now insert in the chart:

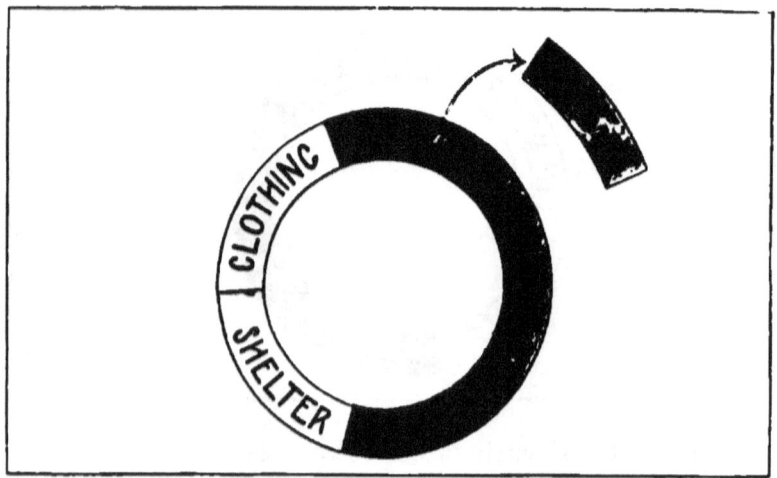

How would the outflow of food affect managers of retail stores? Every merchant's office-boy knows. It would admonish them to order further supplies from wholesalers. Wholesalers would fill these orders, and replenish their stock by ordering from manufacturers. Manufacturers would thereupon send all over the world

---

70. If it be asked how Personal Servants can draw this food out of the retail stores unless they have money, let the questioner inform himself as to the ways in which business is done. No man, unless he be a notorious cheat, needs money in order to obtain goods at retail stores, provided he has or can presently get profitable employment. All he needs is employment, or an early prospect of employment, and a reputation for honesty. There is therefore no unwarranted assumption in the example, even if we exclude the use of money from consideration. See *post*, note 72.

THE LAW OF LABOR.   49

for materials; would call for new machinery and better machinery; would order new buildings and repair old ones, and would scour the country for workingmen to come into their factories and renew their lowered stock of goods. Thus all kinds and grades of labor that could assist in producing food, from farm hands to inventors, from bookkeepers to sailors, would feel the influence of the demand for food in a demand for their labor. What Personal Servants really do in demanding food is to direct the expenditure of labor to the production of food and food-producing implements and materials.

Let us indicate this point upon the chart by running a blue arrow from Food-makers to the food reservoir:

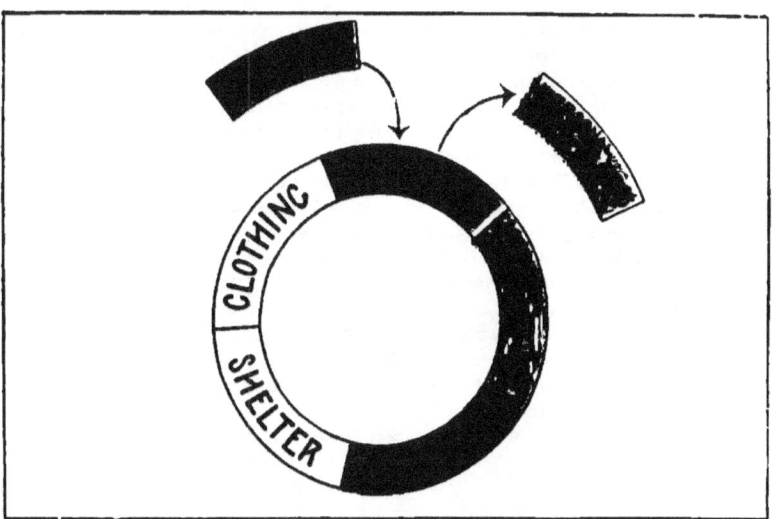

No complaint may now arise of lack of work in food-producing lines.[71] But work is only a means to an end.

[71]. Farmers, millers, bakers, ranchers, butchers, fishermen, hunters, makers of food-producing implements, food merchants, railroad men, sailors, draymen, coal miners, metal miners, builders, bankers who by exchanging commercial paper facilitate trade, together with clerks, bookkeepers, foremen, journeymen, common laborers, and other hired workmen in all these various branches of food production, find work

It is done for the compensation it yields. And how are Food-makers to be compensated? In services from Personal Servants? Suppose they are not in want of services. But they must be in want of something; if they need nothing they have no poverty to relieve. Let it be clothing that they lack. Then they are compensated for making food by taking clothing from retail stores in exchange for their unpaid claim against Personal Servants. Clothing thereupon flows out of the commercial reservoir to them as food flowed out to Personal Servants; and with similar effect, namely, the setting to work of all clothing-making

seeking for them instead of their seeking for work. To specify the labor that would be profitably affected by this demand would involve the cataloguing of all workmen, all business men, and all professional men who either directly or indirectly are connected with food industries, and the naming of every grade of such labor, from the newest apprentice to the largest supervising employer.

Would not this be putting an end to "hard times"? For what is the most striking manifestation of "hard times"? Is it not "scarcity of work"? Is it not that there are more men seeking work than there are jobs to do? Certainly it is. And to say that, is not to limit "hard times" to hired men. The real trouble with the business man when he complains of "hard times" is that people do not employ him as much as he expects to be employed. Work is scarce with him, just as with those he employs, or as he would phrase it, "business is slack."

Let there be ten men and but nine jobs, and you have "hard times." The tenth man will be out of work. He may be a good union man who abhors a "scab" and will not take work away from his brother workman. So he hunts for a job which does not exist, until all his savings are gone. Still he will not be a "scab," and he suffers deprivation. But after a while hunger gets the better of him, and he takes one of the nine jobs away from another man by underbidding. He becomes a "scab." And who can blame him? any one would rather be a "scab" than a corpse. Then the man who has lost his place becomes a "scab" too, and turns out some one else by underbidding. And so it goes again and again until wages fall so low that they but just support life. Then the poorhouse or a charitable institution takes care of the tenth man, who thereafter serves the purpose of preventing a rise in wages. Meanwhile, diminished purchasing power, due to low wages, bears down upon business generally.

But let there be ten jobs and but nine men. Conditions would instantly reverse, Instead of a man all the time seeking for a job, a job would be all the time seeking for a man; and wages would rise until they equaled the value of the work for which they were paid. And as wages rose purchasing power would rise, and business in general would flourish.

If demand freely directed production, there would always be ten jobs for nine men, and no longer only nine jobs for ten men. It could not be otherwise while any wants were unsatisfied.

labor, from sheep-raisers and cotton-growers to sewing-women and salesmen.

The yellow arrows denote this:

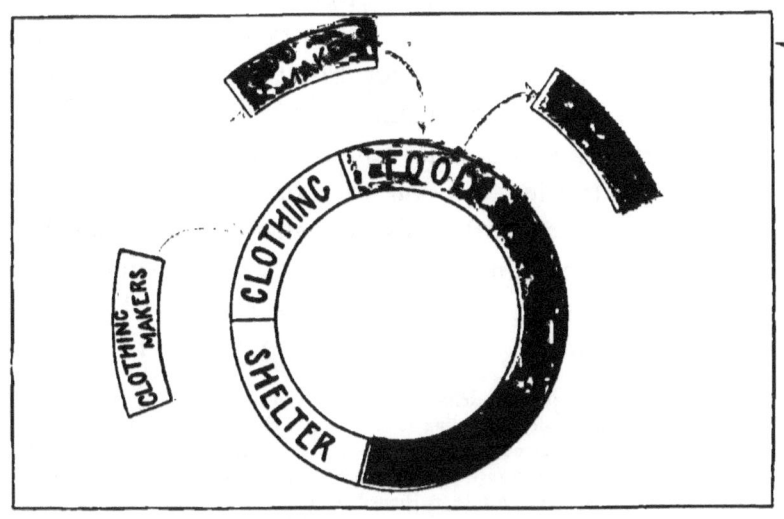

The poverty of Food-makers as to clothing is thus removed. They are working all they care to at food-making, their own chosen employment, and they are paid in clothing, their own chosen compensation. So long as Personal Servants withdraw food and Clothing-makers supply clothing, Food-makers cannot be poor. With them business will be brisk, labor will be in demand, and wages will be high.

That all the other workers may enjoy the same prosperity we shall see in a moment. Clothing-makers pour clothing into the commercial reservoir because they wish to take something out, and know that in this way they can get a larger quantity and better quality of what they require than if they undertake to make it themselves. They are skilled in making clothing; they are not skilled in other ways. Accordingly they utilize the claim against Personal Servants, which has passed to their credit in exchange for clothing, by drawing from the commercial reservoir the particular commodity they desire. Suppose it to be shelter. They proceed as Personal Servants and Food-makers have already done, and so set Shelter-makers at work. Shelter-makers in turn utilize the claim against Personal Servants which has now been credited to them, by taking luxuries out of the reservoir. This sets Luxury-makers at work. Luxury-makers then pass the claim over in exchange for services, and Personal Servants redeem it by rendering such services as Luxury-makers demand.[72] Everybody is now paid for his own

---

72. The mechanism of these exchanges should be explained:

Personal Servants upon demanding food may pay money for it. The retailers might thereupon pass the money along, and it would ultimately return to Personal Servants. Or the Personal Servants may give notes payable at a future time, which being endorsed over would at last be redeemed by them in services. Or they may give checks on banks, which assumes previous work done by them or the discounting of their notes by the banks. As the world's exchanges are almost wholly adjusted by means of checks, and other commercial paper which is in economic effect the same as checks, let us illustrate that mode by a series of charts adapted from Jevons.

We will begin with two traders, A and B. They have no money, but every time that one demands anything of the other he must offer in exchange something that the other wants. There must be what is called "a double coincidence" of demand and supply; each must want what the other has. This is primitive barter. It may be represented by the following chart:

A———————B

In the civilized state, even in its beginnings, primitive barter must be obstructive to trade, and it gives way to the use of currency—some common medium which is taken for goods not because the taker wants it but because he knows that he can readily exchange it for the goods that he does want. With currency in use, when A wants anything of B he is not obliged to find something that B wants. All he needs is currency. Thus currency reduces the friction of trading.

But as the volume of trade augments, demand for currency increases; and because it is scarce, or troublesome or dangerous to transmit, or all together, easier means of exchange are resorted to, and bookkeeping takes the place of currency as currency took the place of primitive barter. At this stage, when A wants anything of B, B charges him; and when B wants anything of A, A charges him. Their mutual accounts being adjusted, the small balance is paid with currency. Thus the demand for currency is greatly lowered by bookkeeping, and the friction of trading is correspondingly reduced.

products with the products of others ; and by demand-

Now let us bring in two more traders, C and D:

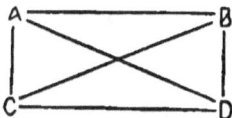

Though all four of these traders keep mutual accounts, the settlement of balances requires more currency than before, and scarcity of currency, together with the danger and expense of transmission, evolves an extension of bookkeeping. A common bookkeeper, called a " Bank," is employed, and all need for currency disappears :

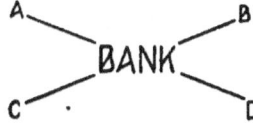

Balances are now settled by checks, and all accounts are adjusted in the central ledger at the bank.

But the introduction of another group of traders, another community, renews the demand for currency, and another bank appears. Thus :

And now the two banks are in the same position that A and B were in before any bank came. They keep mutual accounts, but they must have currency to settle their balances. And if we bring in more communities the demand for currency further increases. Thus :

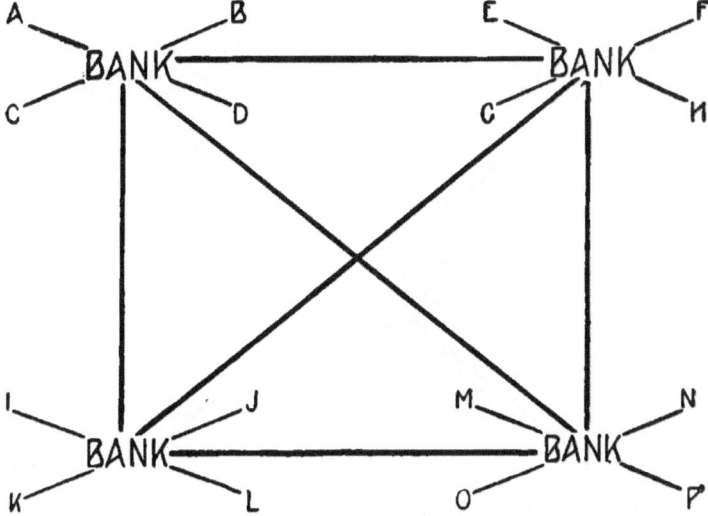

ing more food, Personal Servants may perpetuate the

Now the four banks are in the same situation that A, B, C and D were in before there were any banks. This evolves a bank of banks—a clearing-house:

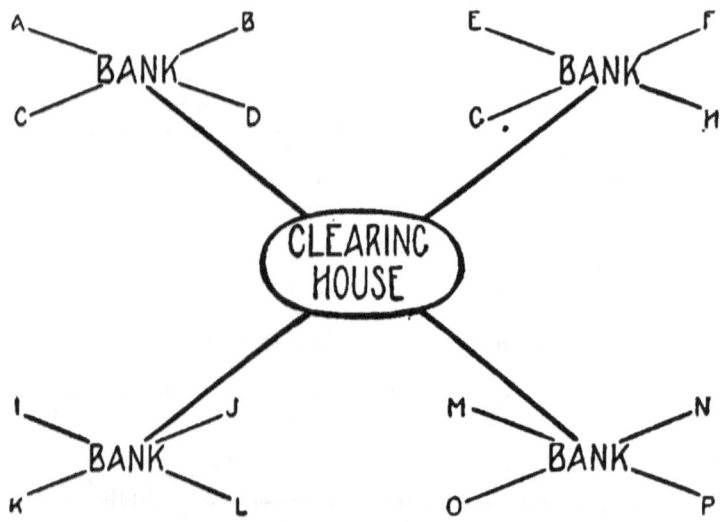

All necessity for currency once more disappears.

These charts illustrate the principle by which mutual trading is effected. In practice, the need of currency is never wholly done away with, but the tendency is constantly in the direction of doing away with it. And it is said that over ninety per cent. of the trading transactions of the world are adjusted in this manner, and less than ten per cent. by means of currency.

The clearing-house principle extends over the civilized world. In illustration of this, observe the following chart:

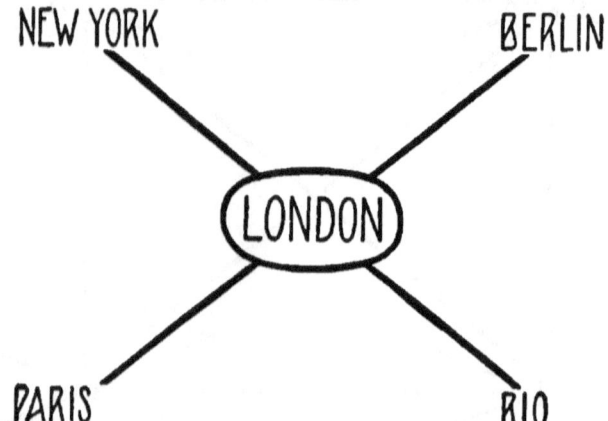

These five cities are like the five banks. The bookkeeping of each city is con-

interchange indefinitely.[73] And Personal Servants will continue to demand more food until their wants as to food are wholly and finally satisfied.[74]

ducted by local banks and clearing-houses, and the central bookkeeping by those of the market town of the world, which at present is London.

In this way the mobility of labor is in effect enormously increased. Labor in every corner of the world is brought into close trading relations with labor everywhere else, so that only war, pestilence, protection, and land monopoly interfere with the full freedom of its movement.

73. Personal Servants, on the basis of their employment by Luxury-makers, demand more food, which keeps Food-makers at work; Food-makers demand more clothing, which keeps Clothing-makers at work; Clothing-makers demand more shelter, which keeps Shelter-makers at work; Shelter-makers demand more luxuries, which keeps Luxury-makers at work; Luxury-makers demand more services, which keeps Personal Servants at work. And so on indefinitely.

If now we add progressive invention, so that every one produces more and more wealth with less and less labor, instead of finding poverty upon the increase, instead of being harried by periodical " hard times," we shall find business brisk and every one becoming richer and richer. That is to say, though all labor less than before, each obtains better results from others while giving better results in exchange.

And should we improve the verisimilitude of the illustration by bringing in the fact that all workers in civilized society are specialists in a much more minute degree than the division into Clothing-makers, Food-makers, etc., would imply—that every one who works does over and over some one thing in one of these branches, as the making of shoes or the baking of bread, or even only part of a thing, as the cutting of shoe soles, and that while giving out a great deal of his own product he demands in pay a little of every other kind of product—the same effect would naturally result.

Every man who demands anything for consumption thereby determines the direction of labor toward the production not only of that thing, but also of all the artificial materials and implements, from the simplest tool to the most expensive and complex machine, that are used in its production. The actual process is much more intricate than that of the charts, but the charts illustrate the principle so that any intelligent person who understands them can apply it to the most complex affairs of industrial life.

" This principle is so simple and obvious that it needs no further illustration, yet in its light all the complexities of our subject disappear, and we thus reach the same view of the real objects and rewards of labor in the intricacies of modern production that we gained by observing in the first beginnings of society the simpler forms of production and exchange. We see that now, as then, each laborer is endeavoring to obtain by his exertions the satisfaction of his own desires; we see that although the minute division of labor assigns to each producer the production of but a small part, or perhaps nothing at all, of the particular things he labors to get, yet, in aiding in the production of what other producers want, he is directing other labor to the production of the things he wants—in effect, producing them himself. And thus, if he makes jackknives and eats wheat, the wheat is really as much the produce of his labor as if he had grown it for himself and left wheat-growers to make their own jackknives."—*Progress and Poverty*, book i, ch. iv.

74. There is no end to man's wants.

" The demand for quantity once satisfied, he seeks quality. The very desires that he has in common with the beast become extended, refined, exalted. It is not merely hunger, but taste, that seeks gratification in food; in clothes, he seeks not merely

Let the chart be now advanced to show, in accordance with the text, the perpetual flow of trade which this action and reaction of demand and supply maintain:

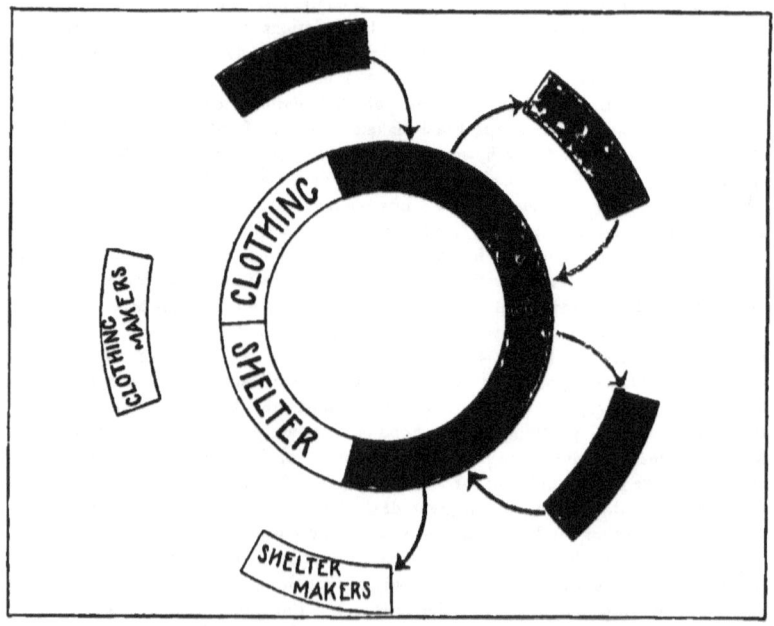

Thus each class of workers by its demands for consumption determines the direction of the labor of some other class. And in final analysis every person by his own demands for consumption determines the direction of his own labor in production as truly as Crusoe determined his; for the demands of Personal comfort, but adornment; the rude shelter becomes a house; the undiscriminating sexual attraction begins to transmute itself into subtle influences, and the hard and common stock of animal life to blossom and to bloom into shapes of delicate beauty."— *Progress and Poverty*, book ii, ch. iii.

A labor agitator was arguing the labor question with a rich man, the judge of his county, when the judge as a clincher asked:

"What do workingmen want, anyway, that they haven't got?"

Promptly the agitator replied with the counter-question:

"Judge, what have you got that you don't want?"

Servants for food, of Food-makers for clothing, of Clothing-makers for shelter, of Shelter-makers for luxuries, and of Luxury-makers for services, by enabling all to procure what they require in exchange for what is demanded of them, determine each as to the kind of employment to adopt.[75]

[75] Regarding society as a unit, the operation of the law is no less indisputable in social than in solitary conditions. The demands of society as a whole determine the degree of activity for each department of production, much as Robinson Crusoe's demand for baskets imposed greater activity upon his arms than upon his legs, or as his demand for goats imposed greater activity upon his legs than upon his arms.

But it is not necessary to regard society as a unit in order to see that in the social as in the solitary state, labor in production is expended in the direction of demand for consumption. Each individual, in the social as in the solitary state, produces the identical wealth that he demands for consumption. The man, for example, who wants a coat, and to get it makes shoes that he does not want, but with which he hires some one to make him a coat, really produces the coat; while he who wants shoes, and to get them makes coats which he does not want but which he trades for shoes, really produces shoes. Similarly, through the whole range of industry, each individual hires other individuals to do what he wants done, and pays for it by doing for others what they want done. The condition is one of reciprocal hiring, and under the common-sense legal maxim, *qui facit per alium facit per se* (what one does by another he does himself), as sound in economics as in jurisprudence, each laborer, by inducing others to make the things that he demands, in order to exchange them for what he makes, really produces what he demands. But for his demands, supplemented by his labor, these things would not be produced.

True it is that in general trade goods are usually made in advance of specific demand for them. But it would be superficial reasoning to infer from this that production determines consumption instead of being determined by it. The collection of commodities in the market is analogous to the collection of water in reservoirs for the accommodation of the inhabitants of cities. Water is so collected in advance of specific demand, not to induce the people to consume water, but because, being accustomed to consuming water, they make a steady demand for it. And this demand determines the supply. There are large reservoirs for large cities and small ones for small cities. So with the commercial reservoir. Stores are filled with goods in advance of specific demand, not to induce demand but in obedience to it. There is an approximate constancy to the demand for wealth, upon which labor relies, and in consequence of which wealth is continually in process of completion. Though orders be supplied from existing stock, the stock is at once replenished in accordance with the demand upon it. And this is equivalent to the proposition that demand for consumption determines the direction in which labor will be expended in production. For it makes no difference in economic principle whether a shoe dealer takes his customer's measure and makes him a pair of shoes, or keeps shoes in stock, and when he sells a pair buys another like them. In either case the shoe dealer is providing shoes pursuant to order. In the one, he anticipates the order and has the goods ready when they are called for; in the other, he obliges his customer to wait until the goods can be made.

Though production may often seem to precede demand, as when goods are stored months in advance of any possible demand for consumption, and may some-

58   OUTLINES OF POST'S LECTURES.

Let us now complete this chart. When we began it a distinction was noted between Personal Servants, who render mere intangible services, and the other classes, who produce tangible wealth. But essentially there is no difference. By referring to the chart and observing the course of the arrows, Food-makers are seen working for Personal Servants precisely as Personal Servants work for Luxury-makers. We may therefore abandon the distinction. This makes it no longer necessary to mention particular classes of products in the chart; it is enough to distinguish the different kinds of labor."[76]   Thus:

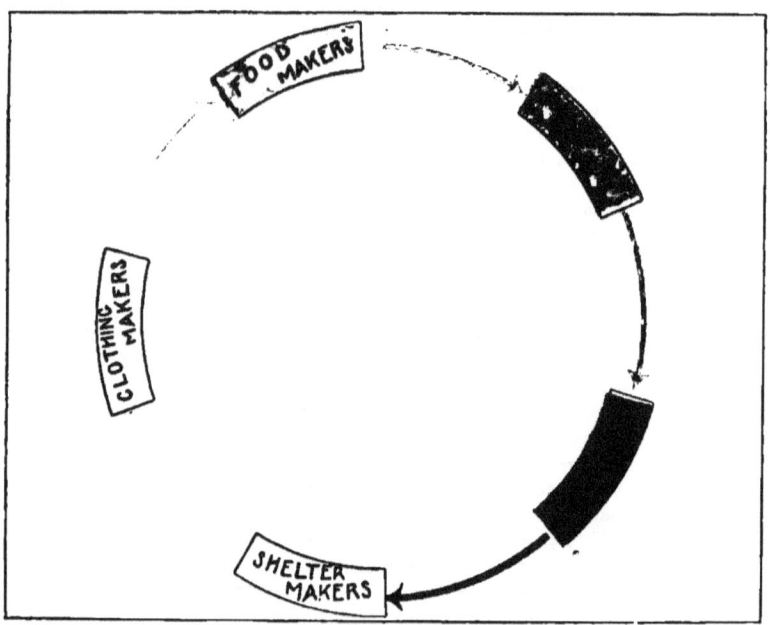

times actually precede it, as when a new nostrum is placed upon the market, the fact remains that production in any direction rises and falls with the rise and fall of demand for consumption ; in other words, is determined by that demand.

And this law regulates the supply of wealth not only as to quantity, but also as to quality and variety.

76. " This, then, we may say is the great law which binds society—' service for service.' "—*Dick's Outlines, p.* 9.

For simplicity the workers have been divided into great classes, and each class has been supposed to serve only one other class. But the actual currents of trade are much more complex. It would be practically impossible to follow them in detail, or to illustrate their particular movements in any simple way. And it is unnecessary. The principle illustrated in the chart is the principle of all division of labor and trade, however minute the details and intricate the movement; and any person of ordinary intelligence who wishes to understand will need only to grasp the principle as illustrated by the chart to be able to apply it to the experiences of every-day industrial life. All legitimate trade is the interchange of Labor for Labor."

d. Dependence of Labor upon Land.

We have now seen that division of labor and trade, the distinguishing characteristics of civilization, not only increase labor power, but grow out of a law of human nature which tends, by maintaining a perpetual

---

77. In the light of this principle how absurd are some of the explanations of hard times.

Overproduction! when an infinite variety of wants are unsatisfied which those who are in want are anxious and able to satisfy for one another. Hatters want bread, and bakers want hats, and farmers want both, and they all want machines, and machinists want bread and hats and machines, and so on without end. Yet while men are against their will in partial or complete idleness, their wants go unsatisfied! Since producers are also consumers, and production is governed by demand for consumption, there can be no real overproduction until demand ceases. The apparent overproduction which we see—overproduction relatively to " effective demand "—is in fact a congestion of some things due to an abnormal underproduction of other things, the underproduction being caused by obstructions in the way of labor.

Scarcity of capital! when makers of capital in all its forms are involuntarily idle. Scarcity of capital, like scarcity of money, is only an expression for lack of employment. But why should there be any lack of employment while men have unsatisfied wants which they can reciprocally satisfy?

Too much competition! when competition and freedom are the same. It is not freedom but restraint, not competition but protection, that obstructs the action and reaction of demand and supply which we have illustrated in the chart.

revolution of the circle of trade, to cause opportunities for mutual employment to correspond to desire for wealth. Surely there could be no lack of employment if the circle flowed freely in accordance with the principle here illustrated; work would abound until want was satisfied. There must therefore be some obstruction. That indirect taxes hamper trade, we have already seen;[78] but there is a more fundamental obstruction. As we learned at the outset, all the material wants of men are satisfied by Labor from Land. Even personal services cannot be rendered without the use of appropriate land.[79] Let us then introduce into the preceding chart, in addition to the different classes of Labor, the corresponding classes of Land-owning interests, indicating them by black balls:

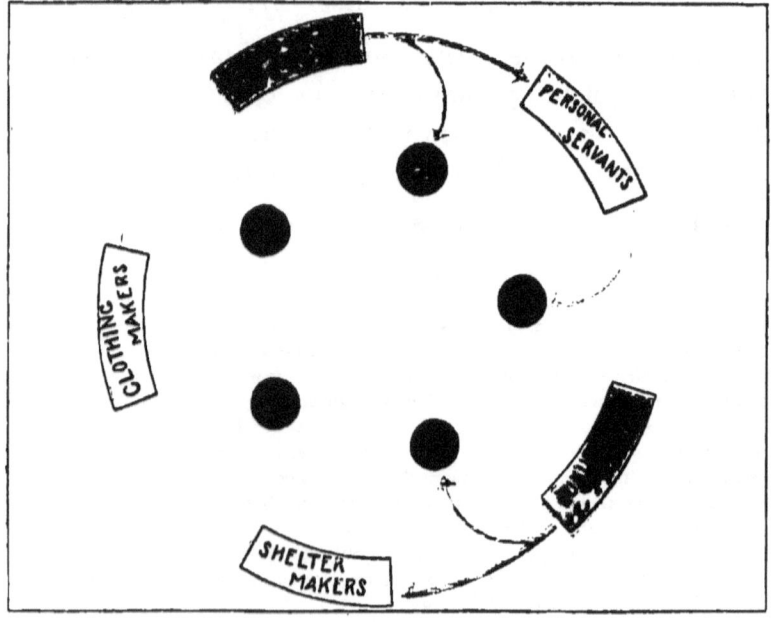

---

78. See *ante, pp.* 5, 6 and 16.
79. Demand for food is not only demand for all kinds and grades of Food-makers,

Every class of Labor has now its own parasite.

The arrows which run from one kind of Labor to another, indicating an out-flow of service, are respectively offset by arrows that indicate a corresponding in-flow of service; but the arrows that flow from the various classes of Labor to the various Land-owning interests are offset by nothing to indicate a corresponding return. What possible return could those interests make? They do not produce the land which they charge laborers for using; nature provides that. They do not give value to it; Labor as a whole does that. They do not protect the community through the police, the courts, or the army, nor assist it through schools and post offices; organized society does that to the extent to which it is done, and the Land-owning interests contribute nothing toward it other than a part of what they exact from Labor.[80] As between Labor interests and Land-owning interests the arrows can be made to run only in the one direction.

Now, suppose that as productive methods improve, the exactions of the Land-owning interests so expand —so enlarge the drain from Labor—as to make it increasingly difficult for any of the workers to obtain the Land they need in order to satisfy the demands made upon them for the kind of Wealth they produce. Would it then be much of a problem to determine the cause of poverty or to explain hard times? Assuredly not. It would be plain that poverty and hard

---

but also for as many different kinds of land as there are different kinds of labor set at work. So a demand for clothing is not only a demand for Clothing-makers, a demand for shelter is not only one for Shelter-makers, a demand for luxuries is not only one for Luxury-makers, a demand for services is not only one for Personal Servants, but these demands are also demands for appropriate land—pasture land for wool, cotton land for cotton, factory land, water fronts and rights of way, store sites, residence sites, office sites, theater sites, and so on to the end of an almost endless catalogue.

80. See *ante*, *pp.* 12, 13, and 14.

tions are due to obstacles placed by Land-owning interests in the way of Labor's access to Land.

We thus see that in the civilized state as well as in the primitive, the fundamental cause of poverty is the divorce of Labor from Land." But the manner in which that divorce is accomplished in the civilized state remains to be explained.

3. The Distribution of Wealth.

The chart on the following page displays the fundamental principle of Production, which we considered at the beginning, and also the fundamental principle of Distribution, which is yet to be considered. In the development of the latter will be found the explana-

but her criticism does not apply to millions of free men who freely trade. To them the land would be enough. Even though they were denied existing roads and ships and bridges and houses, they would soon make new ones, and starting "from where we are," would "go ahead." For free land means access to all natural materials and forces, and free trade means unobstructed industrial intercourse between laborer and laborer. These are the essential conditions, the only conditions, of all production even of the most civilized.

The root of the socialistic idea is the thought that we are dependent for social life upon accumulated capital. This is a mistake. Social life depends, not upon accumulated capital, but upon accumulated knowledge made effective by interchange of labor. A laborer who operates some great machine seems to be dependent upon the owner of his machine for opportunity to work; but the only people upon whom he really depends are laborers who are competent coöperatively to make such machines, and who have access to both the land from which the materials must be drawn and that upon which they must group themselves while doing the work. When socialists lay stress upon the importance of accumulated capital they are attributing to accumulated capital the power that resides in land and trade; for to control these is to command the benefits of accumulated knowledge.

Since the production of a machine precedes its use, the inference is almost irresistible, upon a superficial consideration, that opportunities to labor and compensation for labor are governed by the existing supplies of machinery to which labor is allowed access. But this is of a piece with the old notion of classical political economy that opportunities to labor are dependent upon the existing supplies of subsistence that are devoted to the maintenance of laborers. The inference is wrong in either form. When we once grasp the essential truth of the law illustrated in the text, that the production of subsistence, or machinery, or any other unfinished object, that is to say, of Capital, is but a form of general wealth production, and that all forms of wealth production are in obedience to demand, we clearly see that labor is in no respect dependent upon capital either for employment or compensation. In the actual as in the chirary state, Labor and Land are the only factors of wealth production. It is not Capital but Land that supplies materials to Labor for its subsistence and its machinery. Instead of capitalists supplying laborers with subsistence and machinery, laborers themselves continuously produce subsistence and machinery from the materials that Land supplies. Capitalists neither employ nor pay laborers; laborers employ and pay one another.

Read "Progress and Poverty," book i, chs. iii, iv, and v. Also read "The Story of My Dictatorship" (No. 4, Sterling Library), chs. v, vi, vii, and viii.

tion of the divorce in the civilized state of Labor from Land:

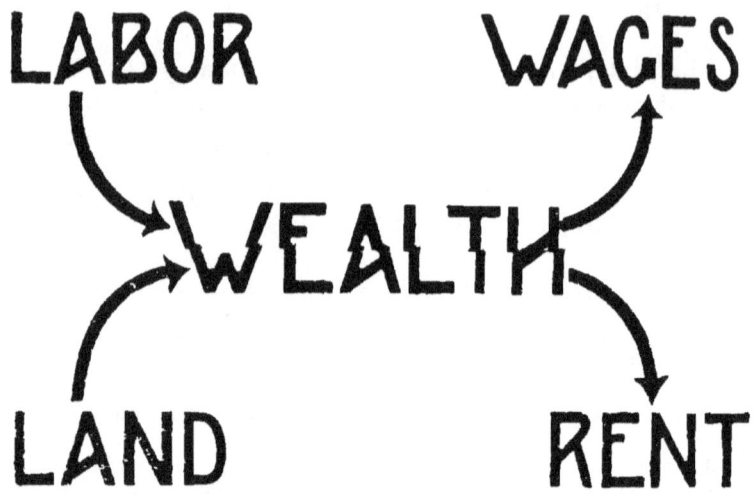

This chart reminds us that Labor (human exertion), by application to Land (natural materials and forces external to man), produces Wealth (the generic term for all those things that tend to satisfy the material wants of man), and so tends to abolish poverty. No man's poverty can be abolished in any other way, unless it be by gifts, or vulgar robbery, or legalized spoils.

The chart shows also that Wealth distributes ultimately in Wages[82] (a fund made up of the aggregate of

---

[82]. "What is paid for labor of any kind is called wages. We are apt to speak of the payment given to the common day laborer only as wages; and we give finer names to the payments which are made for some other kinds of services. Thus we speak of the doctor's or the lawyer's fee; of the judge's salary; of the teacher's income; of the merchant's profit; of the banker's interest, and of the professor's emoluments. They are all in reality only payments for labor of different kinds, or for different results of labor, —that is, they are all wages."—*Dick's Outlines, p.* 23.

"Wages is what goes to pay for the trouble of labor."—*Jevons's Primer, sec.* 39.

"His [the manager's] share is called the wages of superintendence, and although

the *earnings* of individual laborers), which corresponds to Labor; and Rent[83] (a fund made up of the aggregate *premiums* for specially desirable locations), which corresponds to Land.[84]

usually much larger than the share of a common laborer, it is really wages of the same nature."—*Id., sec.* 41.

" The common meaning of the word wages is the compensation paid to a hired person for manual labor. But in political economy the word wages has a much wider meaning, and includes all returns for exertion. For, as political economists explain, the three agents or factors in production are land, labor, and capital, and that part of the produce which goes to the second of these factors is styled by them wages. . . It is important to keep this in mind. For in the standard economic works this sense of the term wages is recognized with greater or less clearness only to be subsequently ignored."—*Progress and Poverty, book i, ch. ii.*

83. Rent " is what is paid for the use of a natural agent, whether land, or beds of minerals, or rivers, or lakes. The rent of a house or factory is, therefore, not all rent in our meaning of the word."—*Jevons's Primer, sec.* 40.

" The term rent in its economic sense . . . differs in meaning from the word rent as commonly used. In some respects this economic meaning is narrower than the common meaning; in other respects it is wider.

" It is narrower in this: In common speech, we apply the word rent to payments for the use of buildings, machinery, fixtures, etc., as well as to payments for the use of land or other natural capabilities; and in speaking of the rent of a house or the rent of a farm, we do not separate the price for the use of the improvements from the price for the use of the bare land. But in the economic meaning of rent, payments for the use of any of the products of human exertion are excluded, and of the lumped payments for the use of houses, farms, etc., only that part is rent which constitutes the consideration for the use of the land—that part paid for the use of buildings or other improvements being properly interest, as it is a consideration for the use of capital.

" It is wider in this: In common speech we only speak of rent when owner and user are distinct persons. But in the economic sense there is also rent where the same person is both owner and user. Where owner and user are thus the same person, whatever part of his income he might obtain by letting the land to another is rent, while the return for his labor and capital are that part of his income which they would yield him did he hire instead of owning the land. Rent is also expressed in a selling price. When land is purchased, the payment which is made for the ownership, or right to perpetual use, is rent commuted or capitalized. If I buy land for a small price and hold it until I can sell it for a large price, I have become rich, not by wages for my labor or by interest upon my capital, but by the increase of rent.

" Rent, in short, is the share in the wealth produced which the exclusive right to the use of natural capabilities gives to the owner. Wherever land has an exchange value there is rent in the economic meaning of the term. Wherever land having a value is used, either by owner or hirer, there is rent *actual;* wherever it is not used, but still has a value, there is rent *potential.* It is this capacity of yielding rent which gives value to land. Until its ownership will confer some advantage, land has no value."—*Progress and Poverty, book iii, chap. ii.*

84. " The primary division of wealth in distribution is dual, not tripartite. Capital is but a form of labor, and its distinction from labor is in reality but a subdivision, just as the division of labor into skilled and unskilled would be. In our examination

a. *Explanation of Wages and Rent.*

Differences in the desirableness of land divide Wealth into the two funds, Wages and Rent. Labor naturally applies its forces to that land from which, considering all the existing and known circumstances, most Wealth can be produced with least expenditure of labor force. Such land is the best. So long as the best land exceeds demand for it, laborers are upon an equality of opportunity, and the entire product goes to them as Wages in proportion to the labor force they respectively expend. But when the supply of the best land falls below demand for it, some laborers must resort to land where with an equal expenditure of labor force they produce less wealth than those who use the best land. The laborers thus excluded from the best land naturally offer a premium for it, or what is the same thing, offer to work for its owners for what they might obtain by working for themselves upon the poorer land. This condition differentiates Rent from Wages. Rent goes to land-owners as such, irrespective of whether they labor or not; Wages go to laborers as such, irrespective of whether they own land or not.[85]

we have reached the same point as would have been attained had we simply treated capital as a form of labor, and sought the law which divides the produce between rent and wages; that is to say, between the possessors of the two factors, natural substances and powers, and human exertion—which two factors by their union produce all wealth."—*Progress and Poverty*, book iii, ch. v.

Care must be taken not to confuse the hire of a house, commonly and legally termed "rent," with economic Rent. House rent is really Wages; it is compensation for the labor of house building. But economic Rent is not compensation for anything; it is simply the premiums for advantages of location.

85. Land of every kind may vary in desirableness from other land of the same kind. Certain farming land, for example, is so fertile that it will yield to a given application of labor two bushels of wheat to every bushel that certain other farming land will yield; and it is obvious that, other things being equal, farmers would prefer the more fertile land. But some fertile land lies so far away from market that less

LAW OF WAGES AND RENT. 67

To illustrate : On the following page are four closed spaces representing land which varies in productiveness to a given expenditure of labor force,[86] from 4 down to 1. There is also an open space at the right, represent-

fertile land lying nearer is more productive, because it costs less to exchange its products for what their producer demands ; in such cases farmers would prefer the less fertile land. The same principle applies to all kinds of land. Building lots at or near a center of residence or business are preferable for most purposes of residence or business to lots equally good in other respects which are far away.

Now, the land that is preferable is of course most in demand ; and if it be all in use, with demand for it unsatisfied, competition for the preference sets in, and gives value to it.

All land cannot be equally desirable. Some excels in fertility. Some is rich with mineral deposits, a species of fertility. On some, towns and cities settle, thereby adding to the productiveness of the labor that uses it, because these sites are thus made centers of co-operation or trade. And yet production in the civilized state requires that the producer shall have exclusive possession of the land he needs. This necessity inevitably gives to some people more desirable land than others have, even though all should have an abundance. Consequently the returns to equal labor are unequal. The man who has land that is more fertile or better located than that of another gets more wealth than the other in return for a given expenditure of labor. If, for example, one with given labor produces 10 bushels of corn from fertile land, equal, say, to $5 worth of any kind of wealth in the market, and the other with the same labor produces 8 bushels of corn, or $4 worth of any kind of wealth in the market, the first receives 2 bushels (or $1) more for his labor than the other receives for his, though each labors with equal effort, skill, and intelligence. Or, if the fertility of the land be the same, but its situation in reference to the market be such that the cost of transportation still preserves the relation of $5 to $4, the same inequality of wages results. It is this phenomenon that gives rise to Rent. Rent is the market value of just such differences in opportunity as are here illustrated. It is a premium for choice land, for preferential locations, for site, for space.

This premium is a very different thing from compensation for labor. Nor is the difference modified when premium owners first obtain Wages for work and with them buy the premium-commanding land. Rent can no more be turned into compensation for labor by exchanging labor products for the power to exact it, than a man can be turned into Wealth by exchanging Wealth for him. Whether the fruits of purchase or of conquest, or of fraud, Rent always constitutes that part of Wealth which is deducted from current production as premiums for superior opportunities for production.

Wages and Rent are both drawn from Wealth, and both go often to the same individual and in the same form of payment, as when a freehold farmer enjoys the use of the grain he raises from more fertile land than his neighbors have, or a city freeholder occupies or receives hire from his house and lot : but Wages flow from Wealth to labor as compensation for production, while Rent flows from Wealth to land-owners in premiums for allowing labor to produce Wealth from superior locations. Wages are appurtenant to Labor ; Rent is appurtenant to Land. It is as laborer that the individual takes Wages, but as land-owner that he takes Rent.

86. A unit of labor cannot be definitely measured save by the value of some labor product. The day's labor of one man may produce less than an hour's labor of another. But for purposes of illustration it is competent to refer to a unit of labor force as an abstraction, intending thereby to denote all the labor of muscle and brain requisite to acquire the necessary knowledge and skill and to produce wealth to a given value from given natural sources.

ing land that is yet so poor as to yield nothing to the given expenditure of labor force. Thus:

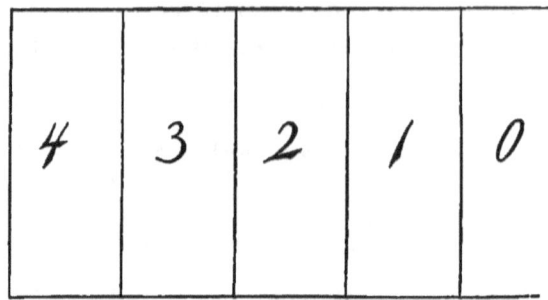

For simplicity let the market be equally convenient to each space. Let it be assumed also that one space is as accessible to labor as another, and that the differences in their productiveness are known. Now, to which space would labor first resort? Obviously to that which would yield most Wealth to the given expenditure of labor force—the space to the extreme left.

Suppose, then, that labor appropriates only as much of the best space as is required for use—say half of it. We may note the fact with red color upon the chart:

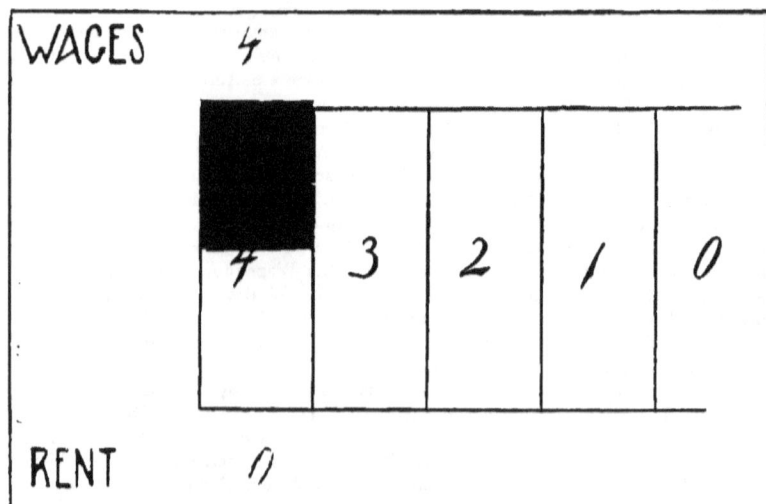

Here we see that Wages are 4 and Rent 0. The laborers, as such, take the entire product, dividing it among themselves in proportion to their services. There is no Rent because other laborers find equally good opportunities to produce in the uncolored part of the space; the supply of the best land exceeds the demand for it, and of course it commands no premium.[87]

But if demand for land should continue until the best space was monopolized,[88] and some laborers were forced to resort to the next, the best space would command a premium;[89] Rent would rise and Wages would

[87] "No land ever pays rent unless in point of fertility or situation it belongs to those superior kinds which exist in less quantity than the demand."—*Mill's Prin.*, book ii, ch. xvi, sec. 2.

"The produce of labor constitutes the natural recompense or wages of labor. In that original state of things, which precedes both the appropriation of land and the accumulation of stock, the whole produce of labor belongs to the laborer."—*Smith's Wealth of Nations,* book i, ch. viii.

"Rent or land value does not arise from the productiveness or utility of land. It in no wise represents any help or advantage given to production, but simply the power of securing a part of the results of production. No matter what are its capabilities, land can yield no rent and have no value until some one is willing to give labor or the results of labor for the privilege of using it ; and what any one will thus give, depends not upon the capacity of the land, but upon its capacity as compared with that of land that can be had for nothing. I may have very rich land, but it will yield no rent and have no value so long as there is other land as good to be had without cost. But when this other land is appropriated, and the best land to be had for nothing is inferior, either in fertility, situation, or other quality, my land will begin to have a value and yield rent. And though the productiveness of my land may decrease, yet if the productiveness of the land to be had without charge decreases in greater proportion, the rent I can get, and consequently the value of my land, will steadily increase. Rent, in short, is the price of monopoly, arising from the reduction to individual ownership of natural elements which human exertion can neither produce nor increase."—*Progress and Poverty*, book iii, ch. ii.

[88] "Rent is the effect of a monopoly; though the monopoly is a natural one, which may be regulated, which may even be held as a trust for the community generally, but which cannot be prevented from existing. . . If all the land of the country belonged to one person he could fix the rent at his pleasure. . . The effect would be much the same if the land belonged to so few people that they could and did act together as one man and fix the rent by agreement among themselves. . . The only remaining supposition is that of free competition."—*Mill's Prin.*, book ii, ch. xvi, sec. 1.

Rent "considered as the price paid for the use of the land is naturally a monopoly price."—*Smith's Wealth of Nations,* book i, ch. xi.

[89] The line of separation between the poorest land thus commanding a premium, and the best land for which labor will not pay a premium, was formerly called "the

fall. Even though but few laborers were forced to the poorer space, they would be perpetual bidders for the advantages of the other space. The effect may be illustrated by indicating with red in our chart the overflow of labor from the first into the second space:

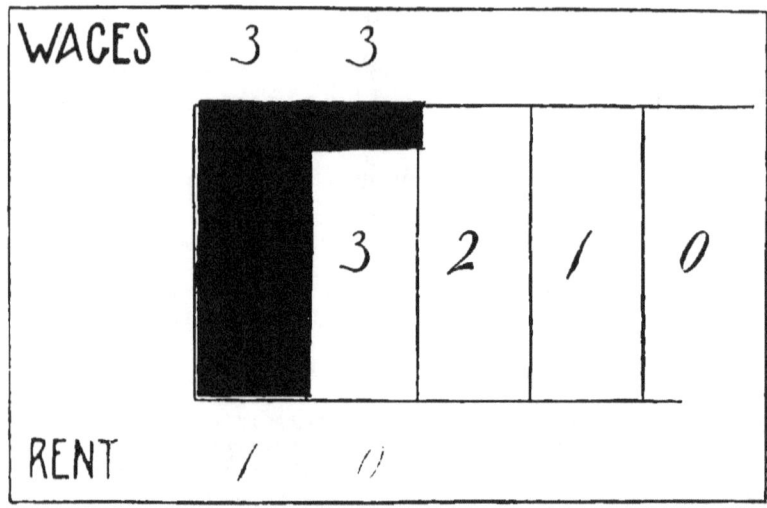

This illustrates the elementary principle of Distribution, that Wages fall and Rent rises as demand for

margin of cultivation," probably because the law of rent was not understood with reference to any but agricultural land ; but it is now more generally called "the margin of production," since it is understood that the law of rent applies to all kinds of land, including, of course, the building lots of cities.

The premium for land falls not into the fund termed Wages, but into the fund termed Rent. Henceforth Wages consist not of the entire product of labor, but of so much of that product as might with the same expenditure of labor force be produced from the best land that commands no premium. The remainder goes to the owners of the land from which it is in fact produced, in proportion to the advantages which their land respectively contributes to its production. This excess is the premium. It is what constitutes Rent as distinguished from Wages. And both the amount of the general fund Rent, and the amount of rent which each land-owner obtains, are determined by the competition of labor for superior opportunities.

Thus, in the beginnings all Wealth would be Wages ; but as labor was forced from better to poorer lands, or, what is the same thing in its principle of operation, as greater capabilities attached to particular lands in consequence of social development, good government, industrial improvement, etc., Rent would arise, and as a proportion of the gross Wealth-product, would increase as labor was forced to poorer land or new

land forces labor to land of lower productiveness.[90] The principle may be more graphically illustrated by supposing that demand for spaces in the chart advances so far as to include all the closed spaces, except part of the poorest one. Thus:

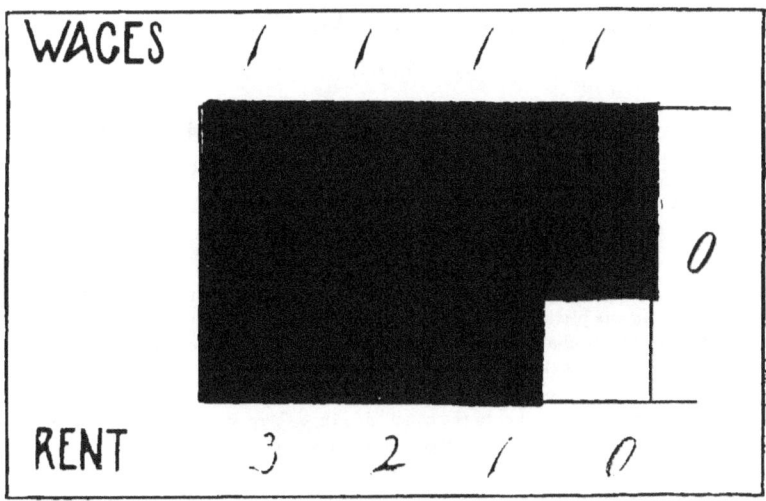

We now find that all Wages have fallen to the level of Wages on the poorest land that yields anything to the given unit of labor force; while the Rent of all but that has, at the expense of Wages, risen in proportion to its superior productiveness.[91]

Reflection will convince us that this must be so. capabilities were added to land by society. The law derived from these phenomena is known as Ricardo's law of rent. Henry George formulates it as follows:

"The rent of land is determined by the excess of its produce over that which the same application can secure from the least productive land in use."—*Progress and Poverty*, book iii, ch. ii.

As will be noticed, the law is the law of Wages as well as the law of Rent. For whatever determines the proportion of Wealth to be taken as Rent necessarily determines the proportion to be left as Wages.

90. Though figures are used, these charts are to be understood not as mathematical *demonstrations*, but simply as *illustrations*.

91. The labor that was forced to the poorest lands would continually bid for the opportunities that the better lands offered, until an equilibrium was reached at the

Wages for a given expenditure of labor force are no more anywhere, for any length of time, all things considered, than the same expenditure of labor force will produce from the best land to be had for nothing. Rent absorbs the difference."[92]

b. *Normal Effect of Social Progress upon Wages and Rent.*

In the foregoing charts the effect of social growth is ignored, it being assumed that the given expenditure of labor force does not become more productive.[93] Let us now try to illustrate that effect, upon

point shown in the preceding chart, where the given expenditure of labor is as well compensated in one place as in another.

If laborer and land-owner be different persons, the laborer receives what is distinguished as Wages, and the land-owner what is distinguished as Rent. If the same person, he receives Wages as laborer and Rent as land-owner.

92. But we must not jump to the conclusion that there is any essential wrong in Rent. Rent is nature's method of measuring the value of the differences in natural opportunity which different laborers, owing to variations in land, are obliged to accept. And, what in practice is more important, it is nature's method of measuring the value to each individual of those advantages which consist in accumulations of common knowledge, in co-operative effort, in good government, in a word, in the benefits that society as a whole confers as distinguished from those which each individual earns. The question is not one of the rightfulness or the wrongfulness of Rent. Personal freedom necessitates Rent, for it necessitates the private possession of land, and private possession of land makes Rent inevitable. Nothing short of communism could abolish it. The real question is, What shall society do with Rent? Shall it give it to individuals, or use it for common purposes?

" Were there only one man on earth, he would have a right to the use of the whole earth.

" When there is more than one man on earth, the right to the use of land that any one of them would have, were he alone, is not abrogated; it is only limited. . . It has become by reason of this limitation, not an absolute right to use any part of the earth, but (1) an absolute right to use any part of the earth as to which his use does not conflict with the equal rights of others (*i. e.*, which no one else wants to use at the same time), and (2) a co-equal right to the use of any part of the earth which he and others may want to use at the same time."—*Perplexed Philosopher, p.* 45.

It is in adjustment of this co-equal right that rent occurs.

93. " The effect of increasing population upon the distribution of wealth is to increase rent . . . in two ways: First, By lowering the margin of cultivation. Second, By bringing out in land special capabilities otherwise latent, and *by attaching special capabilities to particular lands.*

" I am disposed to think that the latter mode, to which little attention has been

the supposition that social growth increases the productive power of the given expenditure of labor force as applied to the first closed space, to 100; as applied to the second, to 50; as applied to the third, to 10; as applied to the fourth, to 3, and as applied to the open space, to 1.[94] If there were no increased demand for land the chart would then be like this:

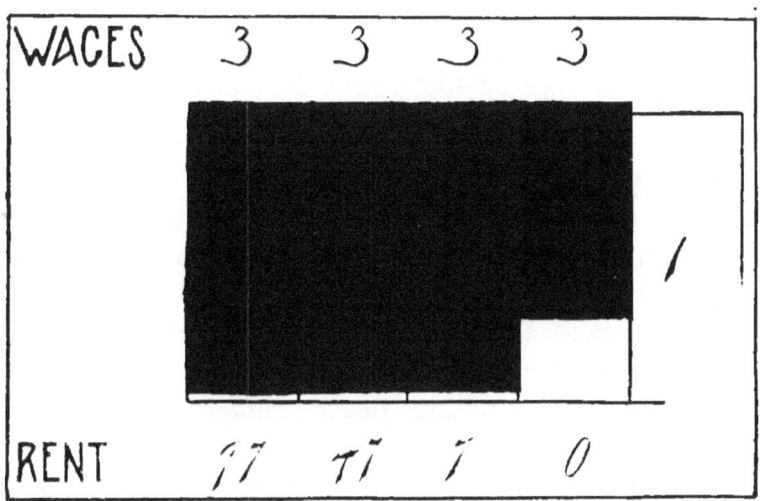

given by political economists, is really the more important."—*Progress and Poverty*, book iv, ch. iii.

"When we have inquired what it is that marks off land from those material things which we regard as products of the land, we shall find that the fundamental attribute of land is its extension. The right to use a piece of land gives command over a certain space—a certain part of the earth's surface. The area of the earth is fixed; the geometric relations in which any particular part of it stands to other parts are fixed. Man has no control over them; they are wholly unaffected by demand; they have no cost of production; there is no supply price at which they can be produced.

"The use of a certain area of the earth's surface is a primary condition of anything that man can do; it gives him room for his own actions, with the enjoyment of the heat and the light, the air and the rain which nature assigns to that area; *and it determines his distance from, and in great measure his relations to, other things and other persons.* We shall find that it is this property of land, which, though as yet insufficient prominence has been given to it, is the ultimate cause of the distinction which all writers are compelled to make between land and other things."—*Marshall's Prin.*, book iv, ch. ii, sec. i.

94. Of course social growth does not go on in this regular way; the charts are merely illustrative. They are intended to illustrate the universal fact that as any land becomes a center of trade or other social relationship its value rises.

Though Rent is now increased, so are Wages. Both benefit by social growth. But if we consider the fact that increase in the productive power of labor increases demand for land we shall see that the tendency of Wages (as a proportion of product if not as an absolute quantity) is downward, while that of Rent is upward.[95] And this conclusion is confirmed by observation.[96]

c. Significance of the Upward Tendency of Rent.

Now, what is the meaning of this tendency of Rent to rise with social progress, while Wages tend to fall? Is it not a plain promise that if Rent be treated as *common* property, advances in productive power shall be steps in the direction of realizing through orderly and natural growth those grand conceptions of both the socialist and the individualist, which in the present condition of society are justly ranked as Utopian? Is it not likewise a plain warning that if Rent be treated as *private* property, advances in productive power will be steps in the direction of making slaves

---

95. "Perhaps it may be well to remind the reader, before closing this chapter, of what has been before stated—that I am using the word wages not in the sense of a quantity, but in the sense of a proportion. When I say that wages fall as rent rises, I do not mean that the quantity of wealth obtained by laborers as wages is necessarily less, but that the proportion which it bears to the whole produce is necessarily less. The proportion may diminish while the quantity remains the same or increases."—*Progress and Poverty*, book iii, ch. vi.

96. The condition illustrated in the last chart would be the result of social growth if all land but that which was in full use were common land. The discovery of mines, the development of cities and towns, and the construction of railroads, the irrigation of arid places, improvements in government, all the infinite conveniences and labor-saving devices that civilization generates, would tend to abolish poverty by increasing the compensation of labor, and making it impossible for any man to be in involuntary idleness, or underpaid, so long as mankind was in want. If demand for land increased, Wages would tend to fall as the demand brought lower grades of land into use; but they would at the same time tend to rise as social growth added new capabilities to the lower grades. And it is altogether probable that, while progress would lower Wages as a proportion of total product, it would increase them as an absolute quantity.

of the many laborers, and masters of a few land-owners? Does it not mean that common ownership of Rent is in harmony with natural law, and that its private appropriation is disorderly and degrading? When the cause of Rent and the tendency illustrated in the preceding chart are considered in connection with the self-evident truth that God made the earth for common use and not for private monopoly, how can a contrary inference hold? Caused and increased by social growth,[97] the benefits of which should be common, and attaching to land, the just right to which is equal, Rent must be the natural fund for public expenses.[98]

If there be at all such a thing as design in the universe—and who can doubt it?—then has it been designed that Rent, the earnings of the community, shall be retained for the support of the community, and that Wages, the earnings of the individual, shall be left to the individual in proportion to the value of his service. This is the divine law, whether we trace it through complex moral and economic relations, or find it in the eighth commandment.

---

97. Here, far away from civilization, is a solitary settler. Getting no benefits from government, he needs no public revenues, and none of the land about him has any value. Another settler comes, and another, until a village appears. Some public revenue is then required. Not much, but some. And the land has a little value, only a little; perhaps just enough to equal the need for public revenue. The village becomes a town. More revenues are needed, and land values are higher. It becomes a city. The public revenues required are enormous, and so are the land values.

98. Society, and society alone, causes Rent. Rising with the rise, advancing with the growth, and receding with the decline of society, it measures the earning power of society as a whole as distinguished from that of the individuals. Wages, on the other hand, measure the earning power of the individuals as distinguished from that of society as a whole. We have distinguished the parts into which Wealth is distributed as Wages and Rent; but it would be correct, indeed it is the same thing, to regard all wealth as earnings, and to distinguish the two kinds as *Communal Earnings* and *Individual Earnings*. How, then, can there be any question as to the fund from which society should be supported? How can it be justly supported in any other way than out of its own earnings?

d. *Effect of Confiscating Rent to Private Use.*

By giving Rent to individuals society ignores this most just law,[99] thereby creating social disorder and inviting social disease. Upon society alone, therefore, and not upon divine Providence which has provided bountifully, nor upon the disinherited poor, rests the responsibility for poverty and fear of poverty.

Let us try to trace the connection by means of a chart, beginning with the white spaces on page 68. As before, the first-comers take possession of the best land. But instead of leaving for others what they do not themselves need for use, as in the previous illustrations, they appropriate the whole space, using only part, but claiming ownership of the rest. We may distinguish the used part with red color, and that which is appropriated without use with blue. Thus:

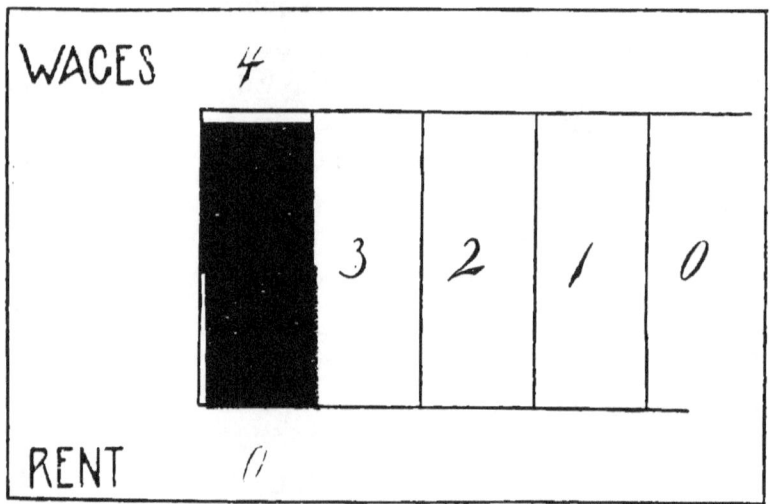

[99] "Whatever dispute arouses the passions of men, the conflict is sure to rage, not so much as to the question ' Is it wise ? ' as to the question ' Is it right ? '

"This tendency of popular discussions to take an ethical form has a cause. It springs from a law of the human mind; it rests upon a vague and instinctive recogni-

SPECULATION IN LAND

But what motive is there for appropriating more of the space than is used? Simply that the appropriators may secure the pecuniary benefit of future social growth. What will enable them to secure that? Our system of confiscating Rent from the community that earns it, and giving it to land-owners who, as such, earn nothing.[100]

Observe the effect now upon Rent and Wages. When other men come, instead of finding half of the best land still common and free, as in the corresponding chart on page 68, they find all of it owned, and are obliged either to go upon poorer land or to buy or rent from owners of the best. How much will they pay for the best? Not more than 1, if they want it for use and not to hold for a higher price in the future, for that represents the full difference between its productiveness and the productiveness of the next best. But if the first-comers, reasoning that the next best land will soon be scarce and theirs will then rise in value, refuse to sell or to rent at that valuation, the newcomers must resort to land of the second grade, though the best be as yet only partly used. Consequently land of the first grade commands Rent before it otherwise would.

tion of what is probably the deepest truth we can grasp. That alone is wise which is just; that alone is enduring which is right. In the narrow scale of individual actions and individual life this truth may be often obscured, but in the wider field of national life it everywhere stands out.

"I bow to this arbitrament, and accept this test."—*Progress and Poverty*, book vii, ch. i.

The reader who has been deceived into believing that Mr. George's proposition is in any respect unjust, will find profit in a perusal of the entire chapter from which the foregoing extract is taken.

100. It is reported from Iowa that a few years ago a workman in that State saw a meteorite fall, and, securing possession of it after much digging, he was offered $105 by a college for his "find." But the owner of the land on which the meteorite fell claimed the money, and the two went to law about it. After an appeal to the highest court of the State, it was finally decided that neither by right of discovery, nor by right of labor, could the workman have the money, because the title to the meteorite was in the man who owned the land upon which it fell.

As the sellers' price, under these circumstances, is arbitrary it cannot be stated in the chart; but the buyers' price is limited by the superiority of the best land over that which can be had for nothing, and the chart may be made to show it:

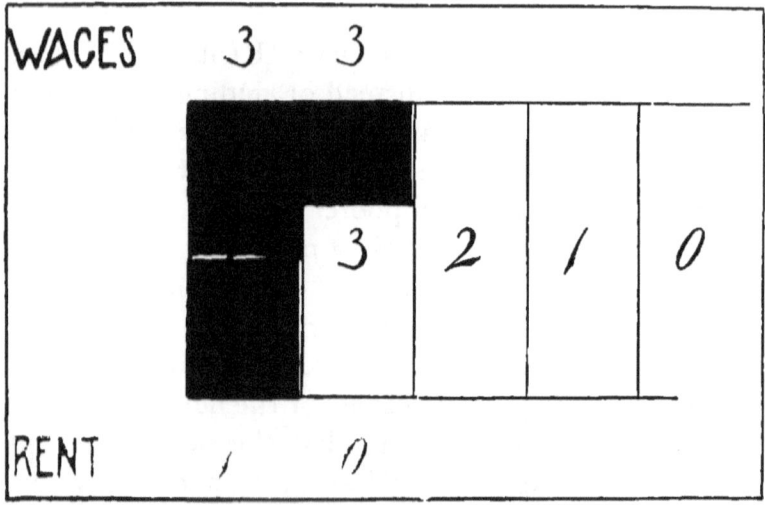

And now, owing to the success of the appropriators of the best land in securing more than their fellows for the same expenditure of labor force, a rush is made for unappropriated land. It is not to use it that it is wanted, but to enable its appropriators to put Rent into their own pockets as soon as growing demand for land makes it valuable.[101] We may, for illustration,

---

[101]. The text speaks of Rent only as a periodical or continuous payment—what would be called "ground rent." But actual or potential Rent may always be, and frequently is, capitalized for the purpose of selling the right to enjoy it, and it is to selling value that we usually refer when dealing in land.

Land which has the power of yielding Rent to its owner will have a selling value, whether it be used or not, and whether Rent is actually derived from it or not. This selling value will be the capitalization of its present or prospective power of producing Rent. In fact, much the larger proportion of land that has a selling value is wholly or partly unused, producing no Rent at all, or less than it would if fully used. This condition is expressed in the chart by the blue color.

"The capitalized value of land is the actuarial 'discounted' value of all the net

suppose that all the remainder of the second space and the whole of the third are thus appropriated, and note the effect:

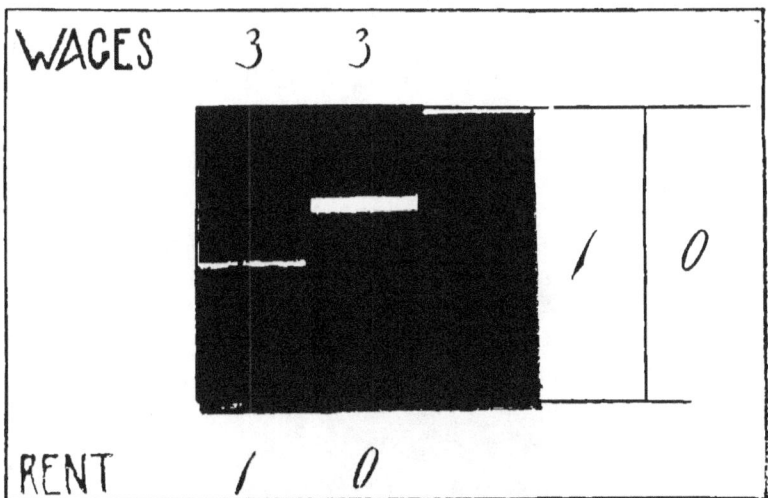

At this point Rent does not increase nor Wages fall, because there is no increased demand for land for use. The holding of inferior land for higher prices, when demand for use is at a standstill, is like owning lots in the moon—entertaining, perhaps, but not profitable. But let more land be needed for use, and matters promptly assume a different appearance. The new labor must either go to the space that yields but 1, or

incomes which it is likely to afford, allowance being made on the one hand for all incidental expenses, including those of collecting the rents, and on the other for its mineral wealth, its capabilities of development for any kind of business, and its advantages, material, social, and æsthetic, for the purposes of residence."—*Marshall's Prin., book vi, ch. ix, sec.* 9.

"The value of land is commonly expressed as a certain number of times the current money rental, or in other words, a certain 'number of years' purchase' of that rental; and other things being equal, it will be the higher the more important these direct gratifications are, as well as the greater the chance that they and the money income afforded by the land will rise."—*Id., note.*

"Value . . . means not utility, not any quality inhering in the thing itself, but a quality which gives to the possession of a thing the power of obtaining other things.

buy or rent from owners of better grades, or hire out. The effect would be the same in any case. Nobody for the given expenditure of labor force would get more than 1; the surplus of products would go to landowners as Rent, either directly in rent payments, or indirectly through lower Wages. Thus:

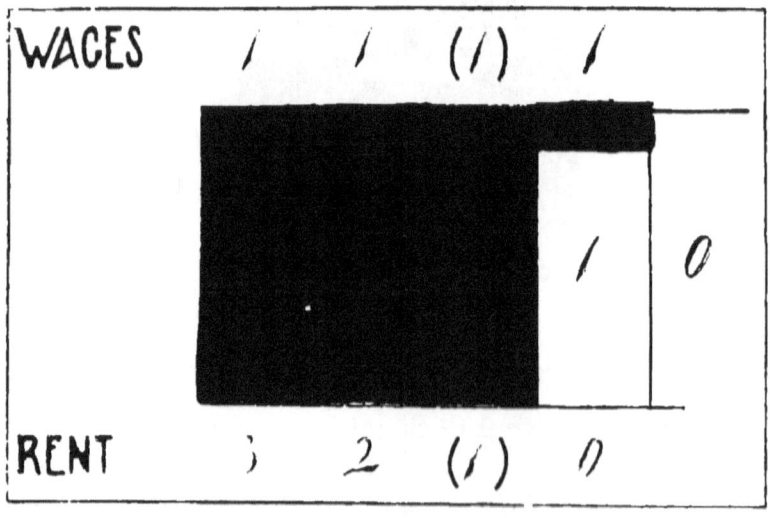

The figure 1 in parenthesis, as an item of Rent, indicates *potential* Rent. Labor would give that much for the privilege of using the space, but the owners hold out for better terms; therefore neither Rent nor

---

in return for it or for its use. . . Value in this sense—the usual sense—is purely relative. It exists from and is measured by the power of obtaining things for things by exchanging them. . . Utility is necessary to value, for nothing can be valuable unless it has the quality of gratifying some physical or mental desire of man, though it be but a fancy or whim. But utility of itself does not give value. . . If we ask ourselves the reason of . . . variations in . . . value . . . we see that things having some form of utility or desirability, are valuable or not valuable, as they are hard or easy to get. And if we ask further, we may see that with most of the things that have value this difficulty or ease of getting them, which determines value, depends on the amount of labor which must be expended in producing them; *i. e.*, bringing them into the place, form and condition in which they are desired. . . Value is simply an expression of the labor required for the production of such a thing. But there are some things as to which this is not so clear. Land is not produced by labor

Wages is actually produced, though but for this both might be.

In this chart, notwithstanding that but little space is used, indicated with red, Wages are reduced to the same low point by the mere appropriation of space, indicated with blue, that they would reach if all the space above the poorest were fully used. It thereby appears that under a system which confiscates Rent to private uses, the demand for land for speculative purposes becomes so great that Wages fall to a minimum long before they would if land were appropriated only for use.

In illustrating the effect of confiscating Rent to private use we have as yet ignored the element of social growth. Let us now assume as before (page 73), that social growth increases the productive power of the given expenditure of labor force to 100 when applied to the best land, 50 when applied to the next best, 10 to the next, 3 to the next, and 1 to the poorest. Labor would not be benefited now, as it appeared to be when on page 73 we illustrated the appropriation of land for use only, although much less land is actually used. The prizes which expectation of future social growth dangles before men as the rewards of owning land, would raise demand so as to make it more than ever difficult to get land. All of the fourth grade would be taken up in expectation of future demand;

yet land, irrespective of any improvements that labor has made on it, often has value. . . Yet a little examination will show that such facts are but exemplifications of the general principle, just as the rise of a balloon and the fall of a stone both exemplify the universal law of gravitation. . . The value of everything produced by labor, from a pound of chalk or a paper of pins to the elaborate structure and appurtenances of a first-class ocean steamer, is resolvable on analysis into an equivalent of the labor required to produce such a thing in form and place; while the value of things not produced by labor, but nevertheless susceptible of ownership, is in the same way resolvable into an equivalent of the labor which the ownership of such a thing enables the owner to obtain or save."—*Perplexed Philosopher, ch. v.*

and "surplus labor" would be crowded out to the open space that originally yielded nothing, but which in consequence of increased labor power now yields as much as the poorest closed space originally yielded, namely, 1 to the given expenditure of labor force."[102] Wages would then be reduced to the present productiveness of the open space. Thus:

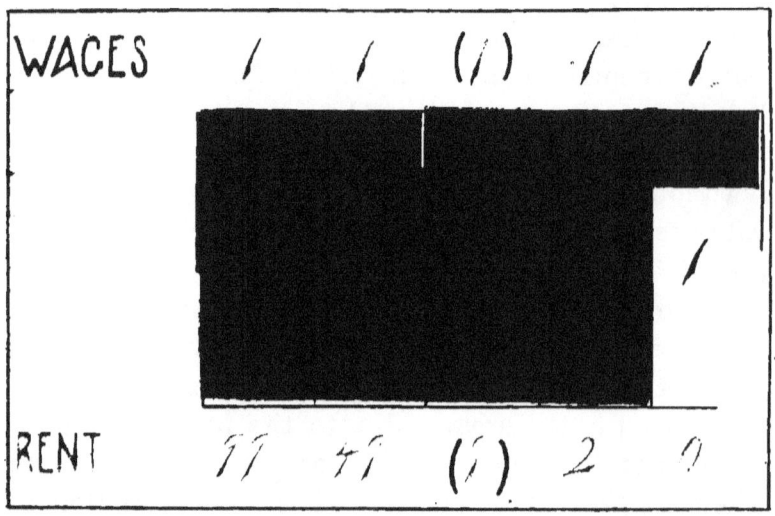

If we assume that 1 for the given expenditure of labor force is the least that labor can take while exerting the same force, the downward movement of Wages will be here held in equilibrium. They cannot fall below 1; but neither can they rise above it, no matter how much productive power may increase, so long as it pays to hold land for higher values. Some laborers

---

102. The paradise to which the youth of our country have so long been directed in the advice, "Go West, young man, go West," is truthfully described in "Progress and Poverty," book iv, ch. iv, as follows:

"The man who sets out from the eastern seaboard in search of the margin of cultivation, where he may obtain land without paying rent, must, like the man who swam the river to get a drink, pass for long distances through half-tilled farms, and traverse vast areas of virgin soil, before he reaches the point where land can be had free of rent—*i. e.*, by homestead entry or preëmption."

would continually be pushed back to land which increased productive power would have brought up in productiveness from 0 to 1, and by perpetual competition for work would so regulate the labor market that the given expenditure of labor force, however much it produced, could nowhere secure more than 1 in Wages.[103] And this tendency would persist until some labor was forced upon land which, despite increase in productive power, would not yield the accustomed living without increase of labor force. Competition for work would then compel all laborers to increase their expenditure of labor force, and to do it over and over again as progress went on and lower and lower grades of land were monopolized, until human endurance could go no further.[104] Either that, or they would be obliged to adapt themselves to a lower scale of living.[105] They in fact do both, and the incidental disturb-

103. Henry Fawcett, in his work on "Political Economy," book ii, ch. iii, observes with reference to improvements in agricultural implements which diminish the expense of cultivation, that they do not increase the profits of the farmer or the wages of his laborers, but that " the landlord will receive in addition to the rent already paid to him, all that is saved in the expense of cultivation." This is true not alone of improvements in agriculture, but also of improvements in all other branches of industry.

104. "The cause which limits speculation in commodities, the tendency of increasing price to draw forth additional supplies, cannot limit the speculative advance in land values, as land is a fixed quantity, which human agency can neither increase nor diminish ; but there is nevertheless a limit to the price of land, in the minimum required by labor and capital as the condition of engaging in production. If it were possible to continuously reduce wages until zero were reached, it would be possible to continuously increase rent until it swallowed up the whole produce. But as wages cannot be permanently reduced below the point at which laborers will consent to work and reproduce, nor interest below the point at which capital will be devoted to production, there is a limit which restrains the speculative advance of rent. Hence, speculation cannot have the same scope to advance rent in countries where wages and interest are already near the minimum, as in countries where they are considerably above it. Yet that there is in all progressive countries a constant tendency in the speculative advance of rent to overpass the limit where production would cease, is, I think, shown by recurring seasons of industrial paralysis."—*Progress and Poverty*, book iv, ch. iv.

105. As *Puck* once put it, "the man who makes two blades of grass to grow where but one grew before, must not be surprised when ordered to 'keep off the grass.'"

ances of general readjustment are what we call "hard times."[106] These culminate in forcing unused land into the market, thereby reducing Rent and reviving industry. Thus increase of labor force, a lowering of the scale of living, and depression of Rent, co-operate to bring on what we call "good times." But no sooner do "good times" return than renewed demands for land set in, Rent rises again, Wages fall again, and "hard times" duly reappear. The end of every period of "hard times" finds Rent higher and Wages lower than at the end of the previous period.[107]

The dishonest and disorderly system under which society confiscates Rent from common to individual uses, produces this result. That maladjustment is the fundamental cause of poverty. And progress, so long as the maladjustment continues, instead of tending to remove poverty as naturally it should, actually generates and intensifies it. Poverty persists with increase of productive power because land values, when Rent is privately appropriated, tend to even greater increase. There can be but one outcome if this continues: for individuals suffering and degradation, and for society destruction.

106. "That a speculative advance in rent or land values invariably precedes each of these seasons of industrial depression is everywhere clear. That they bear to each other the relation of cause and effect, is obvious to whoever considers the necessary relation between land and labor."—*Progress and Poverty, book v, ch. i.*

107. What are called "good times" reach a point at which an upward land market sets in. From that point there is a downward tendency of wages (or a rise in the cost of living, which is the same thing) in all departments of labor and with all grades of laborers. This tendency continues until the fictitious values of land give way. So long as the tendency is felt only by that class which is hired for wages, it is poverty merely; when the same tendency is felt by the class of labor that is distinguished as "the business interests of the country," it is "hard times." And "hard times" are periodical because land values, by falling, allow "good times" to set it, and by rising with "good times" bring "hard times" on again. The effect of "hard times" may be overcome, without much, if any, fall in land values, by sufficient increase in productive power to overtake the fictitious value of land.

e. Effect of Retaining Rent for Common Use.

If society retained Rent for common purposes, all incentive to hold land for any other object than immediate use would disappear. The effect may be illustrated by a comparison of the last preceding chart with the following:

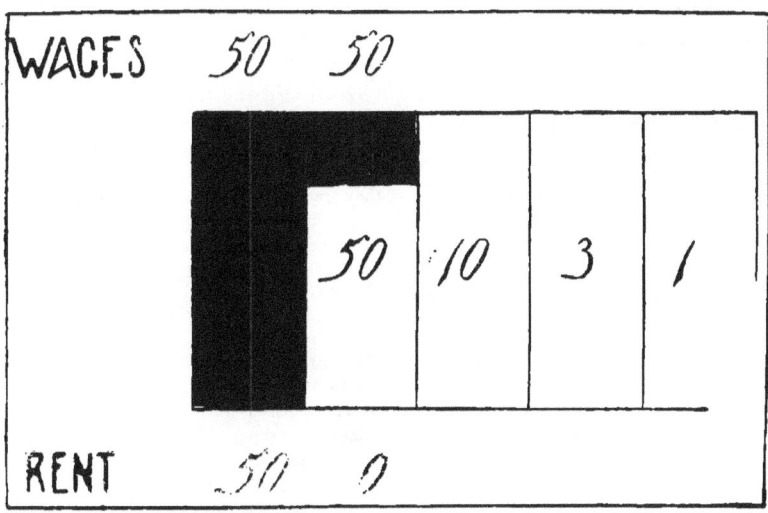

There is but one difference between this chart and the chart immediately preceding. In that Rent is confiscated to private use, whereas in this Rent is retained for common use. All the labor force indicated with red in the first of the two charts would not more than utilize the space to the left and part of the adjoining one, which would elevate Wages to what, with the given labor force, could be produced from the poorer of the two spaces. After that, increase of Rent would not enrich land-owners at the expense of other classes; it would enrich the whole community.[108]

108. The laborer would receive in Distribution all that he earned and no more than he earned in Production; and that is the natural law.

f. The Single Tax Retains Rent for Common Use.

To retain Rent for common use it is not necessary to abolish land-titles, nor to let land out to the highest bidder, nor to invent some new mechanism of taxation, nor in any other way to directly change existing modes of holding land for use, or existing machinery for collecting public revenues. "Great changes can be best brought about under old forms."[109] Let land be

---

In social conditions, where industry is sub-divided and trade is intricate, it is impossible to say arbitrarily what is the equivalent of given labor. Hence no statute fixing the compensation for labor can really be operative. All that we can say is that labor is worth what men freely contract to give and take for it. But it must be what they freely contract to take as well as what they freely contract to give; and men are not free to contract for the sale of their labor when labor generally is so divorced from land as to abnormally glut the labor market and make men's sale of their labor for almost anything the buyer offers, the alternative of starvation. Laborers may be as truly enslaved by divorcing labor from land as by driving them with a whip.

109. "Such dupes are men to custom, and so prone
To rev'rence what is ancient and can plead
A course of long observance for its use,
That even servitude, the worst of ills,
Because delivered down from sire to son
Is kept and guarded as a sacred thing."
 — *Cowper.*

It is only custom that makes the ownership of land seem reasonable. I have frequently had occasion to tell of the necessity under which the city of Cleveland, Ohio, found itself, of paying a land-owner several thousand dollars for the right to swing a bridge-draw over his land. When I described the matter in that way, the story attracted no attention; it seemed perfectly reasonable to the ordinary lecture audience. But when I described the transaction as a payment by the city to a land-owner of thousands of dollars for the privilege of swinging the draw "through that man's air," the audience invariably manifested its appreciation of the absurdity of such an ownership. The idea of owning air was ridiculous; the idea of owning land was not. Yet who can explain the difference, except as a matter of custom?

To the same effect was the question of the Rev. F. L. Higgins to a friend. While stationed at Galveston, Tex., Mr. Higgins fell into a discussion with his friend as to the right of government to make land private property. The friend argued that no matter what the abstract right might be, the government had made private property of land, and people had bought and sold upon the strength of the government title, and therefore land titles were morally absolute.

"Suppose," said Mr. Higgins, "that the government should vest in a corporation title to the Gulf of Mexico, so that no one could fish there, or sail there, or do anything in or upon the waters of the Gulf without permission from the corporation. Would that be right?"

held nominally as it is now. Let taxes be collected by the same kind of machinery as now. But abolish all taxes except those that fall upon actual and potential Rent, that is to say, upon land values.

If that were done it is doubtful if land-owners could any longer confiscate enough Rent to be worth the trouble. Even though some surplus were still kept by them, it would be so much more easy to secure Wealth by working for it than by confiscating Rent to private use, to say nothing of its being so much more respectable, that speculation in land values would practically be abandoned. At any rate, the question of a surplus—Rent in excess of the requirements of the community—may be readily determined when the principle that Rent justly belongs to the community and Wages to the individual shall have been recognized by society in the adoption of the Single Tax.[110]

"No," answered the friend.

"Well, suppose the corporation should then parcel out the Gulf to different parties until some of the people came to own the whole Gulf to the exclusion of everybody else, born and unborn. Could any such title be acquired by these purchasers, or their descendants or assignees, as that the rest of the people if they got the power would not have a moral right to abrogate it?"

"Certainly not," said the friend.

"Could private titles to the Gulf possibly become absolute in morals?"

"No."

"Then tell me," asked Mr. Higgins, "what difference it would make if all the water were taken off the Gulf and only the bare land left."

110. Thomas G. Shearman, Esq., of New York, author of the famous magazine article on "Who Owns the United States," estimates that sixty-five per cent. of the present annual value of the land in the United States would pay all the present expenses of American government—federal, state, county, and municipal.

IV. CONCLUSION.

In " Progress and Poverty," after reaching his conclusion that command of the land which is necessary for labor is command of all the fruits of labor save enough to enable labor to exist, Henry George says:

> So simple and so clear is this truth that to fully see it once is always to recognize it. There are pictures which, though looked at again and again, present only a confused labyrinth of lines or scroll-work—a landscape, trees, or something of the kind—until once attention is called to the fact that these things make up a face or a figure. This relation once recognized is always afterward clear.[111] It is so in this case. In the light of this truth all social facts group themselves in an orderly relation, and the most diverse phenomena are seen to spring from one great principle.

---

111. This idea of the concealed picture was graphically illustrated with a story by Congressman James G. Maguire, at that time a Judge of the Superior Court of San Francisco, in a speech at the Academy of Music, New York City, in 1887. In substance he said:

"I was one day walking along Kearney Street in San Francisco, when I noticed a crowd around the show window of a store, looking at something inside. I took a glance myself and saw only a very poor picture of a very uninteresting landscape. But as I was turning away my eye caught the words underneath the picture, 'Do you see the cat?' I looked again and more closely, but saw no cat in the picture. Then I spoke to the crowd.

"'Gentlemen,' I said, 'I see no cat in that picture. Is there a cat there?'

Some one in the crowd replied:

"'Naw, there ain't no cat there. Here's a crank who says he sees the cat, but nobody else can see it.'

"Then the crank spoke up:

"'I tell you there is a cat there, too. It's all cat. What you fellows take for a landscape is just nothing more than the outlines of a cat. And you needn't call a man a crank either, because he can see more with his eyes than you can.'

"Well," the judge continued, "I looked very closely at the picture, and then I said to the man they called a crank:

"'Really, sir, I cannot make out a cat. I can see nothing but a poor picture of a landscape.'

"'Why, judge,' he exclaimed, 'just look at that bird in the air. That's the cat's ear.'

"I looked, but was obliged to say:

"'I am sorry to be so stupid, but I can't make a cat's ear of that bird. It is a poor bird, but not a cat's ear.'

CONCLUSION.

Many events subsequent to his writing have gone to prove that Henry George was right. Each new phase of the social problem makes it still more clear that the disorderly development of our civilization is explained, not by pressure of population, nor by the superficial relations of employers and employed, nor by scarcity of money, nor by the drinking habits of the poor, nor by individual differences in ability to produce wealth, nor by an incompetent or malevolent Creator, but, as he has said, by "inequality in the ownership of land." And each new phase makes it equally clear that the remedy for poverty is not to be found in famine and disease and war, nor in strikes which are akin to war, nor in the suppression of strikes by force of arms, nor in the coinage of money, nor in prohibition or high license, nor in technical education, nor in anything else short of approximate equality in the ownership of land. This alone secures equal opportunities to produce, and full ownership by each producer of his own product. This is justice, this is order. And unless our civiliza-

---

"'Well, then,' the crank urged, 'look at that twig twirled around in a circle. That's the cat's eye.'

"But I couldn't make an eye of it.

"'Oh, then,' said the crank a little impatiently, ' look at those sprouts at the foot of the tree, and the grass. They make the cat's claws.'

"After another deliberate examination, I reported that they did look a little like a claw, but I couldn't connect them with a cat.

"Once more the crank came back at me. 'Don't you see that limb off there? and that other limb under it? and that white space between? Well, that white space is the cat's tail.'

"I looked again and was just on the point of replying that there was no cat there so far as I could see, when suddenly the whole cat burst upon me. There it was, sure enough, just as the crank had said ; and the only reason that the rest of us couldn't see it was that we hadn't got the right point of view. But now that I saw it I could see nothing else in the picture. The landscape had disappeared and a cat had taken its place. And, do you know, I was never afterward able, upon looking at that picture, to see anything in it but the cat!"

From this story as told by Judge Maguire, has come the slang of the single tax agitation. To "see the cat" is to understand the single tax.

tion have it for a foundation, new forms of slavery will assuredly lead us into new forms of barbarism."[112]

[112] "Our primary social adjustment is a denial of justice. In allowing one man to own the land on which and from which other men must live, we have made them his bondsmen in a degree which increases as material progress goes on. This is the subtile alchemy that in ways they do not realize is extracting from the masses in every civilized country the fruits of their weary toil; that is instituting a harder and more hopeless slavery in place of that which has been destroyed; that is bringing political despotism out of political freedom, and must soon transmute democratic institutions into anarchy.

"It is this that turns the blessings of material progress into a curse. It is this that crowds human beings into noisome cellars and squalid tenement houses; that fills prisons and brothels; that goads men with want and consumes them with greed; that robs women of the grace and beauty of perfect womanhood; that takes from little children the joy and innocence of life's morning.

"Civilization so based cannot continue. The eternal laws of the universe forbid it. Ruins of dead empires testify, and the witness that is in every soul answers, that it cannot be. It is something grander than Benevolence, something more august than Charity—it is Justice herself that demands of us to right this wrong. Justice that will not be denied; that cannot be put off—Justice that with the scales carries the sword."—*Progress and Poverty, book x, ch. v.*

APPENDIX.

BRIEF ANSWERS TO TYPICAL QUESTIONS.

Q. Do you regard the single tax as a panacea for all social disease?

A. When William Lloyd Garrison announced his conversion to the single tax in a letter to Henry George, he took pains to state that he did not believe it to be a panacea, and Mr. George replied: "Neither do I; but I believe that freedom is." Your question may be answered in the same way. Freedom is the panacea for social wrongs and the ills they breed, and the single tax principle is the tap-root of freedom.

Q. Would the single tax yield revenue sufficient for all kinds of government?

A. Thomas G. Shearman, Esq., of New York, estimates that sixty-five per cent. of the rent that the land in the United States now yields actually and potentially to its owners, would be sufficient. But whether it would or not is as yet an unimportant question. If all revenues ought to be raised from land values, then no revenues should be drawn from other sources while any land value remains in private possession. Until land values are exhausted the taxation of labor cannot be excused.

Q. In an interior or frontier town, where land has but little value, how would you raise enough money for schools, highways, and other public needs?

A. There is no town whose finances are reasonably managed in which the land values are insufficient for local needs. Schools, highways, and so forth, are not local but general, and should be maintained from the land values of the state at large.

Q. What disposition would you make of the revenues that exceeded the needs of government?

A. The people who ask this question ought to settle it with those who want to know whether the single tax would yield revenue enough. I do not believe that public revenues under the single tax would exceed the just needs of economical government; in better highways, better sidewalks, better wharves, better schools, better public service of various kinds, we should find sufficient demand for all our revenues. But the question of deficiency or surplus is one to be met and disposed of when it arises. The present question is the wisdom and the justice of applying land values to common use, as far as they will go or as much of them as may be needed as the case may prove to be.

Q. If the full rental value were taken would it not produce too much revenue and encourage official extravagance? If only what was needed for an economical administration of government, would not land still have a speculative value?

A. In the first part of your question you are thinking of a vast centralized government as administering public revenues. With the revenues raised locally, each locality being assessed for its contribution to the state and the nation, there would be no such danger. The possibility of this danger would be still further reduced by the fact that private business would then offer greater pecuniary prizes than would public office, wherefore public office would be sought for purer purposes than as money-making opportunities. As to the second part of your question, the speculative value of land would be wiped out as soon as the tax on land values was high enough and that on improvement values low enough to make production more profitable than speculation. And this point would be reached long before the whole rental value was absorbed in taxation.

Q. If a land-owner builds, does not that increase the value of his land and consequently the amount of the tax he would have to pay? If so, would not he be taxed for his improvement?

A. No. Upon the value of the building he would never pay any tax. It is true that his improvement might attract others to the locality in such numbers as to make land there scarcer and consequently dearer. His own lot would in that case rise in value with the other land and be taxed more, just as the rest would be. But that would not take any of his labor in taxes; he would still have his building free of taxation. Thus: If on a lot worth $1000 a building worth $1000 were erected, making the whole worth $2000, the tax would fall only upon the $1000 which represents the value of the lot. If land then became so scarce that the lot rose in value to $1500 the tax would be raised. But the owner's improvement would be still exempt. When his property was worth $2000 he was taxed on $1000, the value of the lot, leaving $1000, the value of the building, free; and now, though he is taxed on $1500, the value of the lot, $1000, the value of the building, is still free.

Q. If a man owns a city lot with a $5000 building on it, what, under the single tax, would hinder another man, perhaps with hostile intent, from bidding a higher tax than the first man was able to pay, and thus ousting him from his building?

A. The question rests upon a misapprehension of method. The single tax is not a method of nationalizing land and renting it out to the highest bidder. It is a method of taxation. And it would not only hinder, it would prevent the unjust ousting of another from his building. The single tax falls upon land-owners in proportion to the unimproved value of their land; and this value is determined by the real estate market—by the demands of the whole community—and not by arbitrary bids. No one could oust a man from his building by bidding more for the land on which it stood than the occupier was paying; the single tax would not be increased in any case unless the land upon which it fell was in so much greater demand that the owner could let it for a higher rent.

Q. What would be the expense of collecting the single tax as compared with that of collecting present taxes?

A. Much less. It is easier to assess fairly, and easier to collect fully; the machinery of assessment and collection would be simpler and cheaper, and it would not enable first payers to collect the tax with profits upon it from ultimate payers.

Q. How would you estimate land values?

A. As we do it now. As real estate dealers estimate them. As appraisers in partition would estimate them. Read note 28.

Q. How would you value the land of a farm when all the land of the neighborhood was fully improved?

A. By ascertaining the value per square rod of the adjacent highway. The value of that, for the purpose of adding it to the farms along which it runs, would denote the land value of the farms. Read notes 4 and 28.

Q. How can mines be taxed without increasing the price of the out-put?

A. By taxing the royalty, or, what is essentially the same, by taxing their capitalized value as mining opportunities. This would tend to lower rather than increase the price of the product. Read note 11.

Q. How would the single tax be assessed on a railroad which passed through a farm worth (without its improvements) $30 an acre?

A. According to the value, not of the adjacent farms, but of the total right of way, much as the value of a navigable river might be determined if it were private property.

Q. How would you assess the land value tax of a man who, by making levees, had reclaimed land from the Mississippi? Say that the land when reclaimed was worth $50 an acre, but that the levees cost a great deal less.

A. The fact that the levees cost less than the value of the land when reclaimed, shows that the opportunity for reclaiming such land has a value. That value, the value of the opportunity to reclaim, is the land value of the property, and would be the basis of the tax.

Q. How would you adjust mortgages to the single tax scheme?

A. Mortgages are modified deeds, and mortgagees are landowners in degree. I would make no adjustment, but would warn mortgageors and mortgagees to adjust their interests as they see fit when they make their mortgages, just as I would warn buyers and sellers of land to guard their interests as between themselves by their contracts. Full notice has now been given that as soon as possible and as fast as possible we propose to induce the people to bring about a condition in which land values will be taken for public use and improvement values be left for private use. People who in the face of this notice neglect to protect themselves in their contracts have no one else to blame if when the change comes they suffer pecuniary loss in the re-adjustment.

Q. How will the single tax affect leases already made? Will the loss of declining values fall upon the owner or the lessee?

A. That will depend upon the covenants in the lease. It behooves tenants to see to it that their leases contain provisions in this respect. If they fail to protect themselves they cannot complain in case they suffer when the single tax comes into operation. They will have had ample warning, and their misfortune will be due to their own negligence.

Q. Should the whole rental value of land be taken for common use, or only enough for government purposes?

A. Only enough for government purposes. When the people see that this method of taxation improves business, increases wages, cheapens land, and generally promotes prosperity, they will not hesitate to increase their taxes so long as public improvements are needed and land values are unexhausted. As is said in " Progress and Poverty " (book viii, ch. ii): " When the common right to land is so far appreciated that all taxes are abolished save those which fall upon rent, there is no danger of much more than is necessary to induce them to collect the public revenues being left to individual landholders."

Q. How would the tax be collected from those who neglected or refused to pay?

A. As individuals may now collect rent from tenants who refuse to pay: by suing for the tax, or evicting the occupant, or both if necessary. I think, however, that the public would deal more justly with occupants than landlords do with ground renters. I think it would compensate for any loss in respect of improvements.

Q. How would you reach the bondholder, or the man with money alone?

A. Why should we wish to reach him if his bonds or his money represent labor products to which he has honestly acquired a just title? This question is a legitimate offspring of the plundering theory that men should be taxed according to their ability to pay, the merits of which are considered on pages 7-9. It is a question which may also have been suggested by the fact that "bondholders" and "men of money" are so often men who have special privileges which coin money for them. There is a feeling that it would be unfair to allow such special privileges to escape taxation. It would be. But inquiry will show that the most important of these privileges rest in the ownership of land, and that the "bondholders" and "men of money" whom the questioner probably has in mind, are in fact great landlords; that is to say, that their fortunes are really based upon land. When land values were taxed, the great source of unearned incomes—land monopoly—would be practically abolished, and bondholders and men of money would be only those who earn what they have. Such property no man of honest instincts should wish to expropriate.

Q. In your lecture you tell of a meteorite which a poor man found, but which the law gave to the owner of the land on which it fell. (See note 100.) Wouldn't the owner, or possessor, or whatever you choose to call him, of that land get the meteorite just the same if the single tax were in force ?

A. Yes, if only one meteorite fell upon his land. But if meteorites got into the habit of falling there the land would grow in value, and then the single tax would operate to take the value of those meteorites for common use, less the labor expended upon them, the value of which would go to the laborer. I told of the one meteorite to illustrate a principle. But as a practical question we need deal only with land upon which, speaking in metaphor, meteorites have a habit of falling. The occasional diamond, the nugget of gold, or other valuable thing found here or there as one of the accidents of a day, are of no practical moment; it is the diamond fields, the gold mines, the fertile farming spots, the centers of trade, and similar valuable opportunities for labor, that are of moment as factors in social problems.

Q. Would not the single tax increase the rent of houses ?

A. No. It takes taxes off buildings and materials, thus making it cheaper to build houses. How can house rent go up as the cost of building houses goes down ? Read pp. 5 to 8 and the related notes.

Q. Do not the benefits of good government increase the value of houses as well as of land?

A. No. Houses are never worth any more than it costs to reproduce them. Good government tends to diminish the cost of house building; how, then, can good government increase the value of houses? You are confused by the fact that houses, being attached to land, seem to increase in value, when it is the land and not the house that really increases. It is the same mistake that a somewhat noted economic teacher, who advocates protection as his specialty, made when he tried to show that there is an "unearned increment" to houses as well as to lands. He did so by instancing a lot of vacant land which had risen in value from $5000 to $10,000, and comparing it with a house on a neighboring lot which, as he said, had also increased in value from $5000 to $10,000. At the moment when he wrote, the house to which he referred could have been reproduced for $5000; and had he been capable of thinking out a proposition he must have discovered that it was the lot on which the house stood, and not the house itself, which had increased in value.

ANSWERS TO QUESTIONS. 97

Q. What difference would it make to tenants whether they paid land rent to the community or to private owners?

A. When they pay it to the community they are paying it in part to themselves, and what others pay they share in; for they are part of the community. They are also exempt from taxes. And since there would be no inducement to speculate in land if rent went to the community, land would be more plentiful and rents would consequently be lower.

Q. Would not the merchant shift his land value tax by adding it to the price of his goods?

A. No. Read note 11.

Q. Would not the tax on land values increase the value of land?

A. No. Read note 11.

Q. What good would the single tax do to the poor? and how?

A. By constantly keeping the demand for labor above the supply it would enable them to abolish their poverty.

Q. Hasn't every man who needs it a right to be employed by the government?

A. No. But he has a right to have government secure him in the enjoyment of his equal right to the opportunities for employment that nature and social growth supply. When government secures him in that respect, if he cannot get work it is because (1) he does not offer the kind of service that people want; or (2) he is incapable. His remedy, if he does not offer the kind of service that people want, is either to make people see that they are mistaken, or go to work at something else; if he is incapable, his remedy is to improve himself. In no case has he a right to government interference in his behalf, either through schemes to make work, or by bounties or tariffs.

Q. Would working people, whose savings are in savings banks or insurance companies which own land or have mortgages upon land, lose by the shrinkage in land values?

A. Not if the companies were managed intelligently. Well managed companies would shift their investments as they observed the persistent decline of land values. They would do it even as soon as conditions appeared which would naturally cause land values to shrink. But working people could well afford to give all their savings for the permanent employment and high wages that the single tax would bring about. It is not working people but idle people who would lose anything by the single tax.

APPENDIX.

Q. If taxes have to be paid by labor, what difference does it make to laborers whether they are levied in proportion to land values, or otherwise?

A. When taxes are levied upon earners in proportion to earnings, they take what the earners would otherwise keep; but when they are levied upon land-owners in proportion to land values, they take what the earners must in any event lose.

Q. Under the single tax could employers cut wages to the starvation point?

A. No. Under the single tax employers would be constantly bidding for workmen, instead of workmen constantly bidding for employers as is the case now. It is the "oversupply" of labor that makes starvation wages possible, and the single tax would abolish that; not by reducing the supply of labor, the Malthusian device, but by allowing the effective demand for labor to freely increase.

Q. What effect would the single tax have on immigration? Would it cause an influx of foreigners from different nations?

A. If adopted in one country of great natural opportunities, and not in others, its tendency would not only be to cause an influx of foreigners, but also to make their coming highly desirable. Our own experience in the United States, when we had an abundance of free land and were begging the populations of the world to come to us, offers a faint suggestion of what might be expected.

Q. Will not the capitalist be able under the single tax to undersell the laborer—to sell goods for less than cost, at least temporarily—and thereby force him to accept the capitalist's terms?

A. With capitalists continually hunting for men to help them fill their orders, and bidding against each other to get men, as would be the case under the single tax, such a contingency would be in the highest degree improbable. It is practically impossible. Nothing short of a trust, an absolutely perfect trust, of all the owners of capital the world over could produce it. And even then, plenty of very useful land of all kinds being free and labor products being exempt from taxation, all people who were outside of the trust would resort co-operatively to the land, and the trust would be obliged to take them in as the alternative of falling to pieces under their competition.

Q. Is not ownership of land necessary to induce its improvement? Does not history show that private ownership is a step in advance of common ownership?

A. No. Private use was doubtless a step in advance of common use. And because private use seems to us to have been brought about under the institution of private ownership, private ownership appears to the superficial to have been the real advance. But a little observation and reflection will remove that impression. Private ownership of land is not necessary to its private use. And so far from inducing improvement, private ownership retards it. When a man owns land he may accumulate wealth by doing nothing with the land, simply allowing the community to increase its value while he pays a merely nominal tax, upon the plea that he gets no income from the property. But when the possessor has to pay the value of his land every year, as he would have to under the single tax, and as ground renters do now, he must improve his holding in order to profit by it. Private possession of land, without profit except from use, promotes improvement; private ownership, with profit regardless of use, retards improvement. Every city in the world, in its vacant lots, offers proof of the statement. It is the lots that are owned, and not those that are held upon ground-lease, that remain vacant.

Q. Would not the full single tax destroy the basis of all credit—land values?

A. The full single tax—one hundred per cent. of annual ground rent—would wipe out land values, which are but the capitalization of rent. But land values are not the basis of credit. Merchants do not prefer mortgages on land as security for commercial debts, unless they hope to get the ownership of the land through foreclosure. The true basis of every man's credit, from the consumer at the cross-roads store to the great retail merchant at the factory or the jobbing house, is honesty, opportunity, and ability. He who will pay his debts if he can, and has an opportunity to earn enough to pay them with, and is able to make good use of the opportunity, needs no land values to offer as a basis for commercial credit. He has the ideal basis of all credit. And this basis of credit every man could have if the single tax were in operation.

Q. Would the single tax benefit the debtor class? If so, how?

A. It would. By abolishing the monopoly of opportunities to work, and thus enabling debtors to earn enough, while decently supporting themselves, to honestly pay their debts. The debtor class deserves sympathy, not because it is in debt, but because it is forced by existing institutions to go into debt in order to work, and is then so hampered and harried by the same institutions as to make orderly repayment impossible and bankruptcy inevitable.

Q. What would be the effect of the single tax if you still left railroad, telegraph, money, and other monopolies in private hands?

A. The real strength of all monopolies is in land monopoly. Observe, for example, the land holdings of the inside ring of such railroads as the Southern Pacific, to which the interests of the road are corruptly made subordinate. Abolish land monopoly, and the power of all the others will go, as Sampson's strength went with the cutting of his hair.

Q. How is it possible to determine what part of a man's product is due to land, and what part is due to labor?

A. All products are due wholly to the union of land and labor. Labor is the active force, land is the passive material; and without both there can be no product at all. But the part of a man's product that he individually earns, as distinguished from the part that he obtains by virtue of advantageous location, is determined by the law of rent—by what his location is worth.

Q. What is the value of a man's labor?

A. What he can get for it under competition in a free market. There is no other test.

Q. Is there no danger that under the single tax scheming men of great intellect would be able to take advantage of their less intelligent brethren, and by the competitive system corral everything as they do now?

A. If they did, it would not be by the competitive system, but because the competitive system was still imperfectly developed. Competition is freedom, and such a thing as you suggest could not be done where freedom prevailed. I believe that the single tax would perfect competition. If it did, and at any rate to the extent that it did, every one would get what he earned.

Q. Why does not labor-saving machinery benefit laborers?

A. Suppose labor-saving machinery to be ideally perfect—so perfect that no more labor is needed. Could that benefit laborers, so long as land was owned? Would it not rather make landowners completely independent of laborers? Of course it would. Well, the labor-saving machinery that falls short of being ideally perfect has the same tendency. The reason that it does not benefit laborers is because by enhancing the value of land it restricts opportunities for employment.

Q. Under the single tax theory what right have you to tax the value of " made land," like the Back Bay of Boston? Is not such land produced by labor?

A. The surface soil is produced by labor. But the foundation —the bottom of a bay, a swamp, a river, or a hole, is not. " Made land" does not differ economically from a house. Its materials are produced from one place to another and adjusted to meet the demand. But nature in the case of the " made land," as in that of the house, supplies the materials and the foundation. The value of the Back Bay of Boston is chiefly the value of a location —a communal value. The single tax would not take the value of " made land "; it would take the value of the space where the " made land " is.

Q. Why does land tend to concentrate in the hands of the few?

A. Because material progress tends to increase its value, and under existing conditions valuable things tend to concentrate in the hands of the few.

Q. Does not the growth of a community increase the value of other things as well as of land? For example, does it not add to the value of the services of professional men, or of any other business that is dependent upon the presence and growth of the community, as truly as it does to the value of land?

A. Granted that the growth of a community primarily tends to increase profits, the increased profits tend in turn to attract men there to share them. This intensifies competition and tends to lower profits. At the same time it increases demand for land and tends to enhance the value of that. It therefore cannot be said that the growth of a community finally increases the value of other things as well as of land. In fact it does not. Appropriate houses in cities are no dearer than appropriate houses in the country, differences in cost of production being allowed for. And although some professional men get very high wages in thickly populated cities, the average comfort of professional men in cities is no higher than in the country, if as high. Moreover, even if labor values as well as land values were increased by communal growth, it must never be forgotten that labor values must always be worked for by the individual, whereas land values are never worked for by the individual. A lawyer may command enormous fees, but he gets no fee at all unless he works for it; but when land commands enormous rent the owner gets it without doing the slightest work.

Q. Is there any land question in places where land is cheap? In Texas, for example, you can get land as cheap as two dollars an acre. Is there a land question there?

A. There is no place where land is cheap in the sense implied by the question. Land commands a low price in many places, but it is poor land; it is not cheap land. It is true that in Texas there is land that can be had for two dollars an acre, but it would yield less profit to each unit of labor and capital expended upon it than land in New York City which costs hundreds of thousands of dollars an acre. The valuable New York land is the cheaper of the two. The land question is *the* question in every place where land costs more than it is worth for immediate use.

Q. Though some people have made money by owning land, isn't it true that others have lost? And don't the losses more than off-set the gains?

A. Possibly. But that has no bearing upon the question. What men lose through investments in land, the community does not gain; but what they gain the community does lose. Therefore, as between land speculators and the community, the losses cannot be charged against the gains.

Q. What is the difference between speculation in land and in other kinds of property?

A. If all the products of the world were cornered by speculators, but land were free, new products would soon appear and the ill effects of the speculation would quickly pass away. But if all the land were cornered by speculators, though everything else were free, the people would immediately be dependent upon the speculators for a chance to live. That illustrates the difference.

Q. How can it be possible that speculative land values cause business depressions when, as any business man will tell you, the whole item of land value—whether ground rent or interest on purchase money—is one of the smallest items in every business?

A. You overlook the fact that the item of speculative rent is the only item which the business man does not get back again. The cost of his goods, the expense of clerk hire, the rent of his building, the wear and tear of implements, are all received back, in the course of normal business, in the prices of his goods. Even his ground rent, to the extent that it is normal (*i. e.*, what it would be if the supply of land were determined alone by land in use, and not affected by the land that is held out of use for higher values), comes back to him in the sense that his aggregate profits are that much greater than they would be where ground rent was less. But the extra ground rent which he is obliged to pay, in consequence of the abnormal scarcity of land, is a dead weight; it does not come back to him. Therefore, even if infinitesimal in amount, as compared with the other expenses of his business—and that is by no means admitted—it is the one expense which may break a thriving business down. Besides, it is not alone the ground rent paid by the business man for his location that bears down upon his business prosperity; the weight of abnormally high land values in general presses upon business in general, and by obstructing the flow of trade forces the weaker business units to the wall. It is not altogether safe to deduce general economic principles from the ledgers of particular business houses.

Q. Which is the more important, land or money?

A. This is like asking whether to a thirsty man water or a cup is the more important. Land is a necessity; money is but a convenience. The use of money is to facilitate trade. But we can live without trade. And even to trade, money is not indispensable. Trade can be carried on by means of primitive barter or by bookkeeping, and in a very high degree it is so carried on. But we cannot so much as live, either in solitude or in society, without appropriate land. "Give me all the money in the world," said an objector once, "and you may have all the land." And this was the answer: "The first thing I should do would be to order you to give me your money or get off from my land."

Q. Would you let money escape taxation, and so favor money lenders?

A. It is a curious fact that this question is most popular among people who clamor for cheap money. How they expect to cheapen money by taxing its lenders on their loans is past finding out. To tax money lenders is to discourage money lending, and thereby to increase interest on loans. Yes, we should let money escape taxation. It escapes taxation now, which in itself is a politic reason for exempting it; but we should exempt it (by taxing nothing but land values) for the additional and better reason that a man's money is his own and the community has no right to it, while a man's land value is the community's and the man has no right to it. This would not favor money lenders in any invidious sense. It would favor both lenders and borrowers; borrowers by enabling them to borrow on easier terms, and lenders by making their loans more secure.

Q. Would the single tax abolish interest?

A. I do not think so. Interest properly understood is a form of wages, and so far from abolishing it, the single tax, which would tend to increase all forms of wages, would tend to increase interest. But monopoly profits are often confounded with interest, and by force of association have given to interest a bad name; these would be minimized if not wholly abolished by the single tax. It is impossible to answer this question intelligibly to everyone who asks it, without requiring him to be specific; for it is seldom that two persons agree as to what they mean by interest. The Western farmer thinks of the high rate that he pays, partly for risk, partly from his ignorance of the *modus operandi* of banking, and partly because legitimate banking facilities are scarce in his community; the Wall Street operator thinks of the premiums that he pays for currency in times of stress to tide him over from day to day; others think of "interest" on government bonds, and others of dividends of companies with valuable land rights. None of these payments are really interest, and the single tax would tend to rid society of them. But that advantage which the workmen enjoy whose implements and materials are already gathered, over those who have yet to devote time to gathering implements and materials, an advantage which is expressed in money and as interest upon capital, will not, I should think, be abolished by anything that man can do. The value of such an advantage is part of the wages of the labor that creates it.

Q. Would not the single tax take away the home place, and so tend to crush out the home sentiment?

A. When the home place now becomes valuable, it is parted with.

Q. Yes; but when the home place is parted with now, the home owner is compensated by the high price he gets.

A. Then your question does not turn upon the home sentiment but upon the dollar sentiment. As a matter of sentiment, the condition would be no worse in any case than now, and in many cases far better; as a matter of dollars, the question is one of justice and not of the home. Under the single tax any one who wanted a home could have it, and never be obliged to abandon one home for another, unless such changes took place in the neighborhood as to make the place inappropriate for a home. He could not then, as he does now, play dog in the manger, saying to the community, "I will not use this place for appropriate purposes, nor will I allow any one else to do so."

Q. Is not the right of ownership of a gold ring the same as the ownership of a gold mine? and if the latter is wrong is not the former also wrong?

A. If it be wrong for you to own the spring of water which you and your fellows use, is it therefore wrong for you to own the water that you lift from the spring to drink? If so how do you propose to slake your thirst? If you argue in reply that it is not wrong for you to own the spring, then how shall your fellows slake their thirst when you treat them, as you would have a right to, as trespassers upon your property? To own the source of labor products is to own the labor of others; to own what you produce from that source is to own only your own labor. Nature furnishes gold mines, but men fashion gold rings. The right of ownership is radically different.

Q. Is it true that men are equally entitled to land? Are they not entitled to it in proportion to their use of it?

A. Yes, they are entitled to it in proportion to their use of it; and it is this title that the single tax would secure. It would allow every one to possess as much land as he wished, upon the sole condition that if it has a value he shall account to the community for that value and for nothing else; all that he produces from the land above its value being absolutely his, free even from taxation. The single tax is the method best adapted to our circumstances, and to orderly conditions, for limiting possession of land to its use. By making it unprofitable to hold land except for use, or to hold more than can be used to advantage, it constitutes every man his own judge of the amount and the character of the land that he can use.

Q. Is it right that the owners of land should pay all the taxes for the support of public institutions, while the owners of commodities go untaxed?

A. Yes. Public institutions increase the value of land but not of commodities. Read notes 14 and 18.

Q. Our city raises $20,000 for fire protection. Is it fair to tax land, which doesn't get that protection, and let houses go free though they do get it?

A. Is not the land worth more with your fire protection than it would be without it? Which would be better for the owners of land in your city, to pay the $20,000, or to have no fire protection? Read notes 14 and 18.

Q. Rich man with large mansion; poor widow with small house on same sized lot adjoining. The two pay the same tax. Is that right?

A. There is no reason in justice why the community should not charge poor widows as much for monopolizing valuable land as it charges rich men. In either case it confers a special privilege and should be paid what the privilege is worth. The question is seldom asked in good faith. Poor widows who live on lots adjoining large mansions are not numerous, and when they exist they are simply land-grabbers. In our sympathy for these widows, let us not forget the vast armies of widows who not only do not live next to mansions, but have no place in the whole wide world upon which to rest.

Q. If land and labor are equally indispensable factors of production, why are they not equally entitled to the product?

A. The laborer justly owns his labor, but the land-owner cannot justly own his land. The question is not one of the relative rights of men and land, but of men and men.

Q. Should not the poor man be compensated for the loss of his land value?

A. No. The reasons are numerous. Among them are the following: The poor man's rights in the community and in common property are neither more nor less than the rich man's. The better conditions for the poor man which the single tax would bring about would more than off-set his loss in land values. The poor man has no land values worth speaking of.

Q. How would you compensate the man who has bought a lot in order to make a home upon it, but is not yet able to build?

A. By letting him, when he is ready to build, have a better lot for nothing. The single tax would do this by discouraging the cornering of land which now makes all good lots scarce. When land was no longer appropriated except for use, and that would result from the operation of the single tax, there would be an abundance of building lots to be had for the taking, which would be far more desirable than the kind to which men who cannot afford to build homes now resort when they buy lots for a home.

Q. If the value of land be destroyed by the single tax, would not justice require that land-owners be compensated?

A. No. Land is given for the use of all, and rent is produced by the community as a whole. To legally vest land-ownership in less than the whole, excluding those to come as well as those that are here, is a moral crime against all who are excluded. Therefore no government can make a perpetual title to land which is or can become morally binding. Neither can one generation vest the communal earnings of future generations in particular persons by any morally valid title, as they certainly attempt to do when they make grants of land. There is both divine justice and economic wisdom in the command that "the land shall not be sold in perpetuity." In the forum of morals all titles to land are subject to absolute divestment as soon as the people decide upon the change.

Q. If a man buys land in good faith, under the laws under which we live, is he not entitled to compensation for his individual loss when titles are abolished?

A. There is no sounder principle of law than that which, distinguishing the contractual from the legislative powers of government, prescribes that government cannot tie up its legislative powers. Now, land tenures and taxation are so clearly matters of general public policy that no one would deny that they are legislative and not contractual in character. It follows that titles to land, and privileges of more or less exemption from taxation, are voidable at the pleasure of the people. And the possibility of such action on the part of the people is as truly a part of every grant of land as if it were written expressly in the body of the instrument. Moreover, notice was given when Henry George published "Progress and Poverty," and has been reiterated often since in louder and louder tones until the whole civilized world has become cognizant of it, that an effort is in progress to do what is in effect this very thing. That notice is a moral cloud upon every title, and he who buys now buys with notice. It will not do for him when the time comes, to say: " I relied upon the good faith of the government whose laws told me I might buy." He has notice, and if he buys he buys at his peril. Men cannot be allowed to make bets that the effort to retain land values for common use will fail, and then when they lose their bets call upon the people to compensate them for the loss. Read the chapter on "Compensation" in Henry George's "Perplexed Philosopher."

Q. If the ownership of land is immoral is it not the duty of individuals who see its immorality to refrain from profiting by it?

A. No. The immorality is institutional, not individual. Every member of a community has a right to land and an interest in the rent of land. Under the single tax both rights would be conserved. But under existing social institutions the only way of securing either is to own land and profit by it. To refrain from doing so would have no reformatory effect. It is one of the eccentricities of narrow minds to believe or profess to believe that institutional wrongs and individual wrongs are upon the same plane and must be cured in the same way—by individual reformation. But individuals cannot change institutions by refraining from profiting by them, any more than they could dredge a creek by refraining from swimming in it. Institutional wrongs must be remedied by institutional reforms.

OUTLINES

OF

LOUIS F. POST'S LECTURES.

OUTLINES OF THE ECONOMIC LECTURES
DELIVERED IN THE PRINCIPAL CITIES OF
THE UNITED STATES AND CANADA, BY
LOUIS F. POST, OFFICIAL LECTURER OF THE
SINGLE TAX LEAGUE OF THE UNITED STATES,

CONTAINING THE COLORED CHARTS

USED BY HIM,

MAILED POSTPAID ON RECEIPT OF PRICE.

Cloth-bound copies, each, - One Dollar.
Paper-bound copies, each, - Fifty Cents.

Address: THE STERLING PUBLISHING CO.,
106 FULTON STREET,
NEW YORK CITY.

BOOKS BY HENRY GEORGE.

A Perplexed Philosopher.
  12mo, cloth, $1.00; paper, 50 cents.

Progress and Poverty.
  12mo, cloth, $1.00; paper, 50 cents.

Social Problems.
  12mo, cloth, $1.00; paper, 50 cents.

Protection or Free Trade?
  12mo, cloth, $1.00; paper, 50 cents.

The Land Question.
  Paper, 20 cents.

Property in Land. A Controversy with the Duke of Argyll.
  Paper, 20 cents.

The Condition of Labor. An Open Letter to Pope Leo XIII.
  12mo, cloth, 75 cents; paper, 30 cents.

Property in Land, The Condition of Labor, and The Land Question, bound together in one volume. 12mo, cloth, $1.00; paper, 50 cents.

For sale by all booksellers, or sent postpaid on receipt of price.

STERLING PUBLISHING COMPANY,

Sole publishers in the U. S. of Henry George's Books.

106 FULTON STREET, NEW YORK.

www.ingramcontent.com/pod-product-compliance
Lightning Source LLC
Chambersburg PA
CBHW021943160426
43195CB00011B/1199